Writing with Light

Writing

A Simple Workshop in Basic Photography

with Light

By PAUL CLEMENT CZAJA

The Chatham Press, Inc.
Riverside, Connecticut

This book is dedicated to
the memory of my father,
William Czaja,
an artist who taught me how
to perceive light, a man who showed
me how to love all the good that it revealed.

SBN 85699-068-X
Library of Congress Catalog Card Number: 72-93261

Printed in the United States of America
by The Murray Printing Company

Contents

Introduction

ome time ago you were born into life, and by now ou have grown used to existing. You were born to eeing too, and if I'm not mistaken, you are by now more or less accustomed to seeing things all day long and thinking little of it. That's natural, I guess, although there is a problem with getting too used to things; you begin to take them for granted, and what you take for granted you probably don't get the most from.

You have a birthday every year just to celebrate the fact that you were born. To *really* celebrate your birthday is to fully understand all the wonder in that unbelievable happening—your coming into the life that you are. There is a joy in this awareness that lasts longer than birthday cake.

The same should be true of your seeing. Even though you have been seeing things all your life, you are never too old to *really* begin to see — to see more consciously. "Perceive" is perhaps a better word to use than "see," since it better suggests taking hold of

something fully and absorbing it into yourself in order to know it. While it is true that you can also perceive things by touching, tasting and hearing, you especially perceive things by seeing.

When you find a rock whose weight and texture make you want to handle it over and over again, you can put it in your pocket and carry it with you. When you have perceived something with your eyes that you want to keep, you can photograph it.

To photograph something means to write it down with light. The word "photograph" comes from the ancient Greek *photos*, which means light, and *grapho*, to write. The word *grapho* originally meant to engrave or scratch into rock, and thousands of years ago that's what humans did to record something for keeps — they scratched it into rock. Since then, we have discovered how to write using a brush, crayon, pencil, pen and typewriter. It has been only recently that we have learned how to write with light.

I can remember being at the beach with some

7

friends one summer when I was a boy. It was the beginning of our vacation, a time for the first shedding of street clothes for the freedom of bathing suits. At the end of the day we happened to notice that, when an adhesive bandage fell off a friend's arm, the perfect shape of the bandage remained stark white against the beginning tan of the rest of his skin.

This gave us a great idea. The next day we returned with rolls of adhesive tape and scissors. It didn't take us long to have taped on our backs not only the letters of our names, but all sorts of designs; a skull and crossbones, a seagull with outstretched wings, and even a humpbacked dragon with a forked tongue.

We spent more time with our bellies on the sand than in the water, but we felt it was worth it. After three days of tanning we pulled off all the tape and revealed a collection of decorated backs. We thought they were terrific. Although we didn't realize it then, we had made our first photographs: we had written with light on our very own skin.

You, of course, can make your first photographs just as we did. But if you are already tanned, or if you would rather not make a display on your skin, you can also create your first photographs on any good-sized live and growing green leaf. Don't pick it off the plant. Simply tape what you like on the side facing the sun and wait about a week. When you carefully remove the adhesive tape you will find a white image of it remains. When you have an image you like, if you don't think the plant will be hurt by your taking its leaf, snip it off and press it to dry between the pages of a heavy book. If you've done your art work well, you'll have a lasting and unusual creation, written with light.

As you can now see, all you need to make a photograph are four things: light; something sensitive to light; an image you want to capture; and that personal touch which allows you and the rest of the world to know that this was perceived and celebrated by you alone — by you personally. That's what photography is all about: it is a celebration of your seeing.

1. Light

Everyone knows that to see and then to photograph requires light. The problem for you as a beginning photographer, however, is that you not only need light, you have to get to know it well: you have to become very aware of it; you have to begin to really see it, or as we said before, you have to begin to perceive it. As a photographer, light is what you are going to be writing with; it is going to be your pencil or your paint brush, so you will have to know more about it than the simple fact that you need it.

Since the day you were born you found light all around you, and just like your seeing, it has become so much a part of your life that it doesn't surprise you any more. If you are going to become a good photographer, you are going to have to work at changing that; light is going to have to surprise you once again.

At night when our earth turns away from the sun and you turn out your bedroom lamp, it is more than likely that you don't even miss the light that is gone. You just go to sleep and turn through all the hours of darkness unknowingly, until you wake up to a new day of light without care or wonder. You will know that you are becoming a photographer when you begin to *miss* light as it is going away, miss its not being there enough sometimes. You will be a *good* photographer when you begin to take hold of the light that is there both with your eyes and with your feelings, and when you begin to care and wonder about it.

The first thing to notice about light is its *source*, or where it is coming from. The best way to do that is simply to squint your eyes almost shut and look around in a complete circle. Do it right now and you will probably notice at least one bright center, maybe two or three or more. These bright centers you have found are the sources of light around you at this moment. Maybe there is a light bulb at your desk, another across the room in the corner, and perhaps a day-bright window as well, all pouring light at you and at everything around you.

Squint your eyes almost closed again and this time

4

all around you at the same time. There is not just one "light," but many individual lights, each with its own beginnings and its own particular qualities.

This may be unnecessary to point out, but light is just like any other substance that really exists. It is more than just a word: it is something, and it is moving, and it affects other things it meets along the way. Not only are the burning bulb and the burning sun real, but the light that leaves them and travels across the space of the room or the space of the universe is also very real. Light itself is a real thing.

But like the wind which you never see except on the things it causes to move, you can't really see light except on what it touches. From whatever it touches, it bounces into your eyes, giving you the gift of sight. An important quality of light is that it is a giver.

Even though you can't see light itself, you can usually see its source — the burning wire in the bulb — and you can sometimes see its path in reflecting bits of dust in the air of a room.

Every kind of light is itself *energy,* and part of a vast ocean of energy in which everything exists. As a photographer you will have to know and work with this mysterious power called energy, so let's begin to understand at least a little bit about it.

Whenever a substance begins to change its form, it lets free some of its "life force," which is energy. For instance, when a log burns and changes to ash and smoke, energy is freed in the heat we feel and in the flame we see. All kinds of fires are burning all through the universe, in big ways and in little ways, and all

compare the light that is coming from each of the sources you've found. Which one is giving out the most light to you? That's your *prime source,* the one that's helping you most to see. In my case right now, the brightest source is the window light, even though it is the farthest away. Its light is the brightest because its fire is the biggest. The fire in the light bulb is closer; it is right here on the desk. But the light coming in through the window is from the biggest fire we have, our sun. Its light, bouncing in after traveling millions of miles, comes from such a powerful source that we are not able to look directly at it without seriously injuring our eyes. You can squint at the sun's light bouncing off the sky, but don't ever squint at the sun.

So you see, light can come from a number of sources

kinds of energy forces are being freed from them. Every one of the freed forces travels away from its source in a straight, pulsating line, just as ripples in a pond move away from a splash caused by a thrown rock.

These energy forces differ in the size of their ripples and in the distance between the ripples. The smallest energy waves are the deadly penetrating gamma rays feared by astronauts in outer space, and from which we on earth are protected by the thick covering of the atmosphere. These rays pulsate with ripples only four millionths of an inch apart.

The largest energy waves are the invisible radio signals which are picked up by your transistor set and which fill space day and night, indoors and out. The ripples of radio waves are more than six miles apart.

Somewhere in the middle of this vast band of energy is the small family of beams to which our eyes are sensitive. These are the only ones we call *light*. Out of the billions of energy waves radiating through our environment, this small and gentle band of rays has given us sight. No matter whether this kind of energy is released from burning wood, burning candle, burning sun, its wave lengths are similar enough to affect the sensitivity of our eyes so that we react by seeing.

As we already noticed when we were squinting, these sources of light differ in their brightness, or in the amount of their energy. This is caused by the difference in the size of their particular waves, even though their ripples are pretty much the same distance apart.

5

To appreciate the fact that we don't see light itself but, as with the wind, only what it touches, I want you to try three experiments with what I call a *perceptor*. Because our eyes are made so well, we sometimes see too much and notice nothing in particular. Good seeing, and therefore good photography, begins with an awareness of things in particular. Squinting reduces your ability to see so that you can begin to notice important sources of light. With both eyes open, you have a very wide field of vision and your eyes take in a great many objects all at once. A perceptor will help you look at one thing at a time, to see it better, to perceive it.

Making a perceptor is easy. Just take a thin piece of paper and roll it into a tube. Hold it up to one eye, close the other, and you're in business. The cardboard tube from a roll of paper towels is perfect. In a pinch, I just roll up my hand and look through that.

EXPERIMENT 1.

With your perceptor, try concentrating on objects around you, indoors or out, which are being touched by light on one side but not on the other. Zero in on one of them at a time and notice for yourself just what the light is doing to it; where it touches this object first or most, and where the subtle line between the light and shadow happens. Look at different kinds of objects being touched by this same light and see if you can notice how they differ in their ability to reflect light. Do this noticing often and with different kinds of light.

EXPERIMENT 2.

This experiment is a little harder, but you should also try it now. With your perceptor again, study the different objects in front of you and try to notice how each one of them soaks up a different amount of light. Some of them, even though they are in the same sunlight (or bulb light) as the others, hardly reflect any light at all and appear as pitch black as the bottom of a deep hole. Others seem to absorb no light at all, but rather to reflect back every bit that has touched them, and dazzle your eyes nearly as much as the source itself. When you have noticed these extremes, pick out the objects that soak up intermediate amounts of light

and try to grade them with numbers. If zero is something that soaks up all the light and looks totally black and 10 is the number for the source of light itself, how would you rate the other objects as to the amount of light they reflect to your eyes?

This particular method of giving numbers to degrees of reflection was first suggested by the very good and careful photographer, Ansel Adams. He rated the degrees of reflection according to *brightness value* and distinguished them as we did above, calling them *zones* of light. Noting the zones of reflecting light with his light meter and perceiving them with his eye undoubtedly helped make him an outstanding photographer, and I am sure it will help you.

EXPERIMENT 3.

The third experiment I want you to try will take a little more patience. Single out some special object which you enjoy looking at. Examine it carefully with your perceptor in the sun's light at three different times of day: as early in the morning as possible, again at noon, and finally at twilight, when we are almost turned away from our sun. Discover what these three different moments of sunlight can reveal to you about the same object. Do this exercise often, too, with different kinds of objects.

Using your perceptor in these ways will help you begin to be surprised by light again, and to give light meaning in your world of seeing; certainly a fine beginning in photography.

2. Shadow

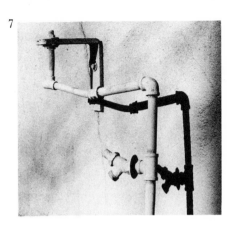

7

Besides having an awareness of light and what it shows us, we should also be conscious of *shadow*. It is just as real and its presence is always felt by us whenever we see anything. In fact, we cannot see something completely unless we see some of its shadow, too. When an object is lit up from every side so that we cannot see any of its shadow, it looks very unreal.

Shadows are a natural part of solid things which light doesn't pass through. The light is stopped and reflected off them, to reveal their images to you and leave their dark shadow-shapes behind them.

Shadows are simply shapes, and can be fascinating on their own, even apart from the objects that have cast them. Begin looking at the particular shadows falling around you right now. Do more than look. "See" each one for a while using your perceptor or your curled hand. Shadows are a little like echoes in that they repeat in a simpler way what is between them and the source of light.

As you know, shadows are fleeting. They change with the light and, of course, disappear without the light. They are hard to take hold of if you like them — especially for keeps. But it is not impossible to capture a shadow for keeps, and I want to teach you a couple of ways before we go any further.

THE SIMPLEST AND OLDEST WAY
TO CATCH A SHADOW

Pick out a small shadow that appeals to you right where you are now. If you can't find a small one to your liking, pick out an interesting part of a big one. Place a piece of blank paper right over the shadow and tape the corners to hold the paper in place, if necessary. While the shadow remains on the paper, trace around it with a pencil or crayon and then cut it out with scissors. By sticking this cutout onto a contrasting piece of paper, you will have a captured shadow-shape to keep. You can then work with shadows of the same object at different times of the day and see the

movement of the sun alter its shape. There's no limit to what you will find.

A MORE MYSTERIOUS WAY TO CATCH A SHADOW

Two hundred years ago a scientist named Johann Schulze accidentally discovered how to make white shadows. One sunny day while in his laboratory, he put a small bottle containing a white-colored solution of acid and silver onto a shelf near his window. Because he was a careful chemist, he had a paper label on the outside of the bottle to identify the contents. He was soon surprised to notice that where sunlight struck his bottle the solution inside turned purple, and where the paper label acted as a barrier to the light rays from the sun, the solution remained creamy white. When he shook the bottle, all the purple disappeared. Fascinated by this happening, Schulze then stuck different cutout shapes on the bottle and put it back into the sunlight. Again the solution of silvered acid began to turn purple everywhere except behind the paper shapes. Since silver in its granular form tends to be a dark purple, he realized that the sun's light (its energy force) was somehow separating or *freeing up* the tiny grains of silver wherever it touched the solution.

Behind the cutouts the solution remained pure, creating, in effect, white "shadows."

It took chemists another hundred years to learn how to improve upon this silver solution and how to coat it onto leather, copper plates, glass plates, paper sheets, and then gelatin film. As with our own skin and sun-greened leaves, man had found something on which to write with light — anything he could coat with silver salt. In fact, I recently read in the newspaper about two young photographers from California who had just figured out a way to coat eggshells with dried silver-salt solution, and they are now printing all kinds of photographs on eggs.

For us to put together all the ingredients for a silver-salt coating would be difficult and even a little dangerous. We'd have to get bars of pure silver, poisonous iodines and powerful acid, just to mention a few. For your first experiments in catching shadows, let's leave that job to the chemists and use the silver-salted paper they have prepared for us. It would be a good idea to read the following steps completely first before carrying them out, to be sure that you understand them.

1. In any convenient camera shop, ask for a package of "slow-acting silver-salted paper," or "photographic paper that can be used for contact printing." Choose a paper size you'd like to work with, and buy a pack with as many sheets in it as you feel fits your budget. As an example, a pack of silver-salted paper with twenty-five sheets each measuring 2½ x 3½ inches would cost you about 50¢. That's two cents a sheet and pretty reasonable, I think.

2. Don't open the pack right away since the paper inside would then be touched by the light energy around you. For the moment, you want to preserve its sensitivity. Before you expose your first sheet to light you ought to plan exactly what you want to make white shadows of, and how you are going to do it.

3. As a first try, I suggest that you simply use your thumb or fingers. Find a corner of a room or a closet where there is as little light as possible. Carefully take one sheet out of the pack and quickly close it tight again. Hold the center of the paper firmly between your thumb and fingers, and bring it out from the dark corner to a source of light. While you are holding it, keep turning both sides of it toward the light. Soon you will find one side begin to change color, and the other side will remain white. The changing side is the smoothest side because it has the silver-salt coating. (Remember this, for some day when you are in a dark-room you will have to tell by touch which side of the paper is which.) When the light has freed up enough silver and darkened the grains enough to satisfy you, take the sheet with your other hand and see what you have accomplished. It will be a white *shadow-graph* either of your thumb or of your fingers.

4. Repeat the experiment with a fresh piece of paper. This time, you decide whether you want a print of your thumb or your fingers or, for a change, whether you want to press something like a key or a leaf tight against the coated side. Keep it exposed to the light until you get a good dark coating of silver.

5. Now try it once more with a third sheet, but this

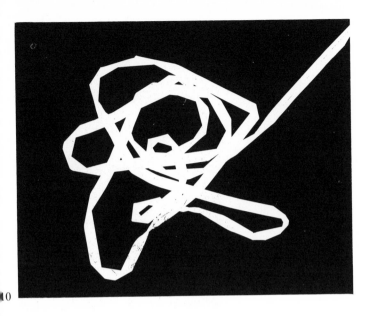

10

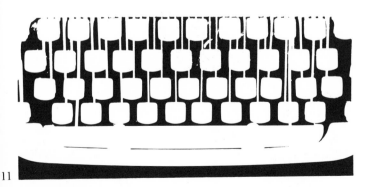

11

time bring your silver-salted paper up to three different light sources, starting with the weakest. For instance, expose it first to lamplight for a minute, then bring it close to a window for a little while, and finally outside into direct sun rays.

You have just used up your first six cents worth of photographic paper, but if things went well, you've learned at least a dollar's worth about writing with light on silver salts.

KEEPING THE WHITE SHADOW WHITE

You will have noticed by now that as soon as you removed your thumb, the leaf or whatever you used to make a white shadow, the light energy present began turning that area dark, too. Before long the entire paper was purplish and your white shadow was gone.

If you have made a shadow-graph that you'd like to keep for more than a little while, you will have to do one of two things. Either hide it from light right away and only peek at it occasionally by candlelight or fix the unexposed silver salts left on the paper so that they have a difficult time getting freed by other light rays.

This second choice is of course preferable, even if it involves a little more work on your part. As soon as you have made a shadow-graph you want to save, put it quickly into a dark place (like your pocket or in between the pages of a closed book) until you can soak it in a bowl of hot water and table salt. It's simple to make a *salt bath* — just fill a dish with hot water and stir in common salt until you see a small layer of it

12

14

22

settling on the bottom. At that point the water should be saturated and ready to do its fixing job. Because table salt is chemically related to silver-salt crystals, they tend to combine and create a light-resistant coating. The process will take a few hours.

The easiest way to dry your shadow-graph and keep it flat is to put it between sheets of paper towel and place a heavy book on top of it overnight.

REVERSING THE SHADOW

When you have properly dried and flattened a white shadow-graph that you particularly like, you may decide that you want to see it reversed — with a dark shape on a pure white background.

1. Take your shadow-graph and pack of light-sensitive paper back into that dark corner.

2. Place a fresh sheet of paper right up against your print, making sure that the sensitized coating faces the image on your shadow-graph. To keep the two papers tightly together during the exposure you can fasten the corners with paper clips or, better still, put them under a pane of clear glass with taped edges.

3. Expose this sandwich to a light source so that the light's energy comes through the back of your original onto the fresh paper. Since the rays will have to go through the thickness of the paper, use the strongest light source available and expect to wait a much longer time for the silver grains on the new print to be freed up and darkened.

4. To know just when your reversed shadow-graph has been exposed long enough to give you the darks

15

and whites you want, you will have to watch the process. Peek in from one corner now and then, but try to keep the two sheets aligned so you won't make a double exposure.

5. When you have the exposure you want, take the new shadow-graph quickly to the hot salt bath to be fixed as you did before.

If you bought a small pack of silver-salted paper a few pages ago and you have been working on these experiments in shadow-graphs, you still should have a dozen or more sheets left. Don't go on to the next page until you've used them all and see how many interesting shadow-graphs you can originate. Use different sizes and shapes of objects; make shadows with objects that let some light through; combine objects and shadows on one print; cast shadows in different directions on the same print; vary the exposures of light and build patterns on your paper; and try exposing different areas of the same paper with different light sources. There are many, many shadow-graphs you can invent that have never been tried before. We can get on with the rest of photography once you've had your fill of shadows.

23

3. A Camera

Capturing the Complete Image

To capture shadows, all you needed was the right kind of light and the right kind of paper. But to capture the complete image of an object itself, you need something more — you need a camera. There's no problem if you don't happen to own a store-bought camera because, for our purposes now, you can make one yourself. In fact, I want to teach you how to make one from things you probably have around you right now.

Just what is a camera, anyway? If we are going to make one, we will need a good model to follow. The fact is, you have two very excellent cameras already in your possession — your eyes! They are living cameras because they are part of your life, but they are cameras just the same.

Since you were a baby your eyes have made your seeing much more than just the capturing of shadows. Things are all around you, and when you open your eyes in light, their images, rich and complete, come pouring into your consciousness. And this miracle happens simply because you are a living camera.

As I grow older I become more and more aware that our world is filled with these miracle-happenings, yet each one of them is simple and obvious to us. Take, for example, a pond turning into ice and then back into water again; or a leaf coming directly out of a woody stem, or a bird floating high on the air alone. Or take the fact that you and I can open our eyes and see reality and care about it. Miracle-happening!

Let's look closely at this seeing and find out just how simply it happens.

Take a minute right now to look closely at one of your eyes in a mirror. What do you notice about it? It's round; there is a dark spot which is actually an opening called the *pupil* right in the center of it; and there is a moveable eyelid over it that lets light in or keeps it out.

But something else must be inside that you can't see in the mirror which reacts to light rays when they come in, something that is as sensitive to light as the silver-salted paper. There is. Inside the center back of the eyeball, there is a patch of light-sensitive nerve cells called the *retina*. If you have ever seen a dog's eyes suddenly shine red at night when they are caught by the lights of a car, then you have had a glimpse of a light-sensitive retina.

Your eye, then, really is another simple kind of miracle; a ball with a hole in it that has light-sensitive material at the back and a lid that can cover and uncover the hole at your command. That's an easy model to copy.

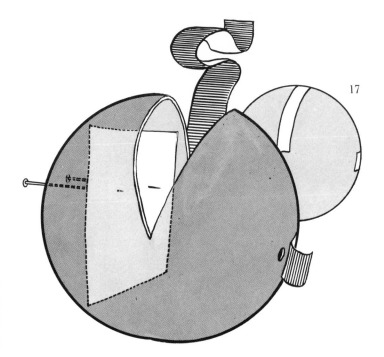

17

A ROUND, RUBBERY AND CHEAP FIRST CAMERA

Whenever you are building something step by step, it is good to read the instructions a few times before actually starting the adventure. You don't want to end up like the man who built a sailboat in his cellar and then could not get it out the door. Making your own camera may not be as grand as constructing a yacht, but it will require the same foresight if you want to be able to use it successfully. So read this section to the end at least once before beginning the project.

1. Find a hollow rubber ball. Any size will do, but of course the bigger the ball, the bigger the photograph. My favorite happens to be an orange beach ball about five inches in diameter. Carefully make a cut halfway around the ball. If you follow the seam it will be easier to keep the slit straight.

2. If you squeeze the ball at the corners of your cut, it will open wide like a mouth so that you can see and get your fingers inside. If your ball is white or shiny inside, see if you can paint it a dull black with shoe

26

polish or a marker pen. You don't want light to be reflecting back and forth off the inside walls when you use it as a camera.

3. If your ball is the kind that is inflated with a needle, you are in luck, for you already have a light hole or *aperture*. You only have to cut off the soft rubber valve that is on the inside to create an opening just the right size. If your ball is not the inflatable kind, you will have to make your own pin hole. In this case, be sure to make your tiny light opening exactly in the center of one of the halves created by your cut. Try to make your pin hole a smooth one and about the size of the letter "o" on this page. If your aperture is too big, the image you capture will be less sharp.

4. This time you won't be making a contact print with light rays pouring directly onto your paper. Instead, you will be letting beams of light which have been reflected off an object come into your camera and you will be limiting the amount of light coming in. It would be good to invest in another pack of silver-salted paper that reacts a little faster than what you used before. Ask in the camera store for "single-weight enlargement paper, grade one or two." Pick a size that will fit easily inside the back of your ball.

5. You will need to have some heavy opaque plastic tape handy to seal up both your aperture and your cut after you put in a piece of light-sensitive paper.

6. Now you must find a really dark corner again, with just enough light by which to see. If you are working at night, use a candle placed a good distance away from you, or use a lamp with a dark red light bulb if you can find one. In the near-dark you can safely take out a piece of your light-sensitive paper and fasten it to the inside back of your ball-camera, directly opposite the pin hole. Make sure you face the coated side of the paper toward the aperture. Remember that the side smoothest to your touch has the silver-salt emulsion on it. To hold your paper to the back of the ball, I recommend that you use two straight pins pushed through from the outside of the ball, pointing toward the aperture and spaced so that you can actually stick the paper onto their points inside the ball.

7. Once the paper is set in your ball-camera, gently seal the slit with one strip of the heavy tape and cover the tiny pin hole with another small piece. Now the ball-camera can take direct sunshine without spoiling the sensitive paper within.

8. If you can't find a suitable ball, you can use any thick cardboard box, or even a coffee can. Be sure to paint the insides black. The important thing is to make a neat, clean pin hole exactly in the middle of one end, and to make sure that the inside is light-tight before and after you make your photograph. Even if you have already made a ball-camera, there's nothing to keep you from inventing others to suit your fancy.

9. Before you go ahead with your pin-hole camera to capture a chosen subject with light, there are a few other important points to consider.

First of all, because you want each beam of light coming from each point on your subject to make a silver mark on only one precise spot on the sensitized paper, you will have to hold the camera perfectly still

18

19

20

28

during the time the light beams are coming in through the aperture. For the same reason, the subject you are photographing must also remain still while you are capturing its reflected image. If your camera moves or if your subject moves, the image on your paper will be blurred. For a beginning it might be good to photograph unmoving, patient, solid things like mountains, rocks or buildings.

Secondly, you will have to figure out just how long to keep the aperture open so that the right amount of light energy comes in to make a satisfactory image. Keep in mind that, although you need a small pin hole to keep your image sharp, a small hole can only let in thin amounts of light energy to each point. So the smaller the hole, the longer you have to expose your paper to the light. Also, since you are dealing with reflected light, the farther away your camera is from your subject, the fewer beams you will be able to capture from each point. And, of course, the weaker the main source of light is, the longer you will have to leave your aperture open.

Actually, the light beams coming in through an average pin hole are so weak that it would take days of exposure before an adequate amount of silver could be freed up to form a visible darkened image on the paper. What can we do about that? We can't always wait around that long for one photograph. The mountain may be patient enough, but we usually are not.

Luckily for us, chemists have discovered that certain chemicals can free up the silver from the silver salt exactly the way light does. Taking some photographic paper already sufficiently struck by light to have freed up a little bit of silver, they soaked it in a solution of these chemicals. Silver grains formed rapidly around this beginning, developing a clear image in a matter of minutes.

In order to photograph something with your ball-camera, all you need to do is let in just enough light to begin freeing up some silver within the paper. Even if you cannot yet see any darkened grains, there will be enough freed up to be "developed" later.

Using my ball-camera I have been able to free up enough silver grains by keeping my aperture open for one, two or three minutes, depending on how much light was available at the time. That's certainly a lot better than waiting for the sun or a strong bulb to do the whole job.

But how do you get your short exposures developed chemically? Well, you have a few choices. Telephone calls to the local YMCA, schools or colleges will often turn up not only a well-equipped darkroom for your use, but also an "expert" to help you in the beginning with the chemicals. If you ask around, you might also discover a camera club, or perhaps even a friend or neighbor who has facilities you would be able to use. And, of course, you could bring your ball-camera with your exposed photographic paper sealed up safe inside to your camera store and ask to have the paper developed there for you. Or, if you prefer, you can hold onto it yourself for a while, and turn to the next chapter so you can learn to make your own darkroom and how to develop your own photographs.

4.
A Darkroom

21

A Private Place in Which to See Again

In my dreams I see again the images my eyes once held on a waking day. Deep in the night the realities that once happened in light somehow come out from the dark cells of my mind and I see them again in new ways within the dark realm of my sleep.

I have always been reminded of seeing dreams when I am in my darkroom bringing out images that are deeply hidden within the atoms of the paper I have briefly exposed. There before my eyes in the semi-dark, as I gently move what looks like blank paper beneath the cool developing solution, an image of yesterday's seeing suddenly reappears like a memory.

Far better than my dream however, which fades away when I awake, the image I develop in my darkroom becomes a new reality in itself. I can hold it in my hand, a now timeless moment of life whose reflection I had written with light on my silver salts carefully and purposefully. Now I have brought it back from another day's time for me to have this day and tomorrow.

This "second act" of photography, which takes place in subdued light with pans of chemicals all about, contains many exciting happenings. Let's start experiencing some of them.

THE ROOM

1. First of all, you will have to find more than a darkened corner. The best place is a room which will hold you and a table or two, but which is roomy enough so you don't go bumping into things in the dark. It is most important that you have a place where you won't be bothered while you are working.

2. Since you will be very much involved with light-sensitive paper, you will have to be able to control the presence of light in your room. Especially if you want to work during daylight, you will have to make sure that no "outside" light can seep in to expose or *fog* your silver salts. As you did with your camera, make sure your room is "light-tight" by taping shut or draping any windows or door cracks. It is much easier

to tell if there are any light leaks within your darkroom than within your camera. All you have to do is stand in the room when the lights are out and look around for four or five minutes in the dark. If there are any leaks, you will notice them quite easily. A darkroom is simply a room which is as dark as you can make it.

3. The silver-salted papers chemists make for us today are prepared so that they are not sensitive to lights which give off only dark, filtered rays. This is done so that you do not have to be in total darkness while you are developing your paper. You can buy such a *safe light* from your camera store. It is not expensive but if you prefer, for a beginning, you can fashion one yourself by taping dark red cellophane over a flashlight, or by using a large red Christmas bulb. Do not try to cover a regular lamp bulb; it will quickly get hot enough to melt or burn paper or cellophane.

4. Because you will be working with liquids, it is convenient but not absolutely necessary to have a source of hot and cold water and a sink. Without doubt you will be dripping something or other onto both table and floor, so you could also use a floor that can take mopping up.

5. It is best to have two tables, at separate sides of the room if possible. One should be kept dry and clean for storing your light-sensitive paper and for working on your photographs. The other should be reserved for the storage of chemicals and for the series of solution trays you will need for developing, fixing and washing your prints.

6. Finally, you will need solution trays and simple tongs. Again, your camera store probably has some of both that are fairly inexpensive, well-made and unbreakable. You will need four trays and three tongs as a very workable minimum. If you want to make do with what you have about the house, you can use old soup dishes or aluminum pans for your trays and spring-type clothespins for tongs. Because you will be using liquid chemicals in your trays that can cause stains, you will need to keep an old towel handy for wiping up spills and drips, as well as a second towel for drying your own hands after washing. Your photographic paper will get annoying spots on it if you go back to the dry table with wet hands.

THE CHEMICALS

Once you have put together a satisfactory darkroom for yourself, you have to prepare a batch of chemicals. To complete the process which the light began for you in your camera you will need four different solutions, each one having a separate job to do.

1. As we mentioned in the last chapter, if enough light energy came in through your pin-hole camera to begin freeing up some silver grains within your paper's coating, even if they cannot be seen, you can amplify them with a special chemical solution. This solution is called *developer,* a word which comes from a French expression meaning "to open like a flower from a bud." This is exactly what these chemical agents seem to do to the light-touched silver grains. They make each one blossom out until they form a

complete image. The photographers of long ago often mixed their own developing chemicals from various elements, but it was a difficult and time-consuming task. Now that there are companies which do all the chemistry for us, you can simply go out and buy what you need. You can select the developing chemicals either already mixed in a liquid solution or, if your prefer, as dry powder that you can dissolve in hot water according to directions on the package. This latter choice is a little cheaper, especially if you buy by the pound and mix up a gallon. To take this route you will also need some large bottles, of unbreakable plastic if possible, a funnel and a measuring pitcher. But if you want to keep matters simple in the beginning, I suggest you skip the mixing for a while and buy a pint of developer already in solution. It won't cost very much and if you pour it back into the bottle after each use, it should last you a good while. Since fresh developing solution is a clear liquid, be sure you mark both your bottle and tray with its name. You don't want to confuse it with your other liquids. As it becomes older and loses its power from use and exposure to air, it will turn a dark coffee brown. Then you will know that it is time to pour it out and buy some more.

2. The chemical action of the developing agents will turn every single one of the silver salts in your paper into dark grains of silver if you give them enough time. Then instead of an image of what you captured with your camera, you would be left with just a piece of black paper. Since, however, these developing agents free the light-struck silver atoms more rapidly than

those that were not touched at all, your image will appear before the remaining salts can be appreciably changed. All you have to do is somehow *stop* the developing action at the moment all the light-struck silver grains appear, and you will have caught your image before it disappears into black shadows. You can do this in one of two ways. The first method comes from common sense: simply pull the paper out of the developing tray at the right moment and wash it with water to get all of the developing solution out of it. About a one-minute rinse usually does the trick. The second way does a more thorough and quicker job. Instead of rinsing the paper in a tray of pure water, add a capful of white vinegar to the water first, making a weak acid solution. This little bit of acid takes the force right out of the developing agents and puts a quick stop to the silver-freeing process. You only have to rinse your print about ten seconds in such a stop bath. Your camera store will also sell you a stop bath solution, usually with a yellow dye added to it that turns purple when the solution becomes worn out. Make sure you clearly mark your bottle of stop solution as well as the tray in which you use it.

3. Two chapters ago you learned the simplest way to fix your shadow-graphs so that your white shadows would stay white: the "old soaking-in-hot-salt-water trick" the first photographers relied on. This process, you remember, tended to complicate the remaining silver salts so much that light had a very hard time breaking the crystals down anymore. As we mentioned, this required a pretty long soaking in the brine

23

and is not always a completely reliable fix. Again the chemists have come up with an ideal solution for us to buy. It is not only quicker but also very thorough in doing its job. They still call it *fixer*, or sometimes *hypo*, but its real name is *sodium thiosulphate*. And what it does is just the opposite of our hot salt-water bath: instead of making the unstruck silver salts into more complicated crystals, this hypo solution very quickly changes them into simpler salts that can wash away in clear water. This then gives us a way to take just about all of the unwanted silver salts out of the paper, leaving the image we have written with light to remain

34

24

by itself indefinitely. So thorough is the fixing of this hypo solution that just a ten-minute soaking can keep your photograph white for centuries of viewing in light. This then should be the third bottle on your darkroom shelf. Mark it clearly, as well as its tray, as fixer.

4. Finally therefore, all you need is lots of fresh water to *wash* your print clean of all the simple salts your hypo has loosened from the emulsion, together with the extra hypo itself. The only problem here is that these remaining salts are invisible and the only way to be sure that they have been completely washed

away is to keep changing the water. Since these salts are heavier than water, they tend to sink to the bottom of your washing tray. There are two good methods of making sure you give your photograph a thorough wash: completely change the water once every two minutes about a dozen times, making sure that your print is kept moving around, and that you drip-drain it before putting it into each fresh bath; or buy a circulating wash tray which keeps refilling as it syphons out the waste salts from the bottom. This latter method is of course easier on you for it does the washing automatically, but it does require running water in your darkroom.

There isn't any real problem if you have no faucet and sink in your darkroom; your fixed prints are safe enough now to be carried out into the light and washed in any sink in your house.

5. Above I mentioned that you will need these four trays of solutions as a "very workable minimum." If, however, you do have the room on your developing table, you could include two additions to the series. First of all, in order to "guarantee" that you get every last one of your unwanted silver salts fixed, it is good to have *two* hypo trays. Soaking your print in the first one for five minutes gets out most of the salts, and then putting it into a fresh solution for the remaining five minutes really finishes them off. This will also leave fewer to be washed out in your fresh-water baths. It is very helpful to add an extra tray of hypo to your string, because when the first batch gets old you can pour it down the drain, replacing it with the fixer

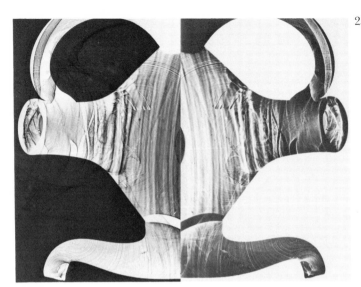

25

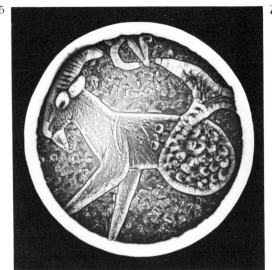

26

27

from your second tray and refilling that one in turn with a fresh solution. This way you will always be sure of soaking your photographs in at least *one* tray of strong hypo.

6. Now for your last extra tray. Since the photographic paper you are using is itself porous and contains tiny fibers, not even twenty hours of washing would get every trace of hypo completely out. This little bit of residue could in time tarnish some of the silver in your image. If you want to make an absolutely permanent print you can, after finishing with the regular water washing, soak your photograph for an additional five minutes in a special solution called *hypo eliminator*. Follow this with a final ten minutes back in the fresh-water wash, and you will have a photograph fixed to the maximum degree.

PUTTING IT ALL TOGETHER

All of this preparation had, as its purpose, bringing out your first photographic print hidden within the paper still closed up in your pin-hole camera. If you have made your own darkroom or located one and it is finally all set up with trays and solutions, let's get in there with your captive image, and shut the door behind us.

1. Right away, put your ball- or box-camera carefully down on the dry table and pour your four basic solutions into their trays (developer, stop, fix or hypo and wash), being sure you don't splash any one into its neighbor. You especially don't want to get any stop or fix into your developer tray for that would put a quick

end to the developing agents. Also be sure to rinse and dry your hands!

2. That done, you can switch on your safe light and turn off your white light, but then wait a few minutes until your eyes adjust to the low light level.

3. Now you can turn back to your camera and open it up. Take out your exposed silver-salted paper, being careful to hold it by its edges so that your fingers do not touch much of the emulsion. It will look as if nothing at all has happened to it since you first put it into your camera. But we know better. Hidden within its atoms is the latent image you have captured. Now carefully slip the paper, emulsion-side down, right into the developer solution. Take hold of one corner of the paper with your developer tongs and turn the paper completely over so that it is now face up, but still submerged in the solution. Let go of it for a while and gently rock the tray with your hand so that the developing solution keeps moving back and forth over the emulsion.

Watch your paper closely for in about half a minute your photograph should suddenly begin to blossom out of nowhere right before your eyes. There is no other experience in photography for me quite like it.

4. The image on your paper will become more and more distinct, and then will reach a peak density and momentarily stop. This is the moment of full development and it is time to remove your print from the developer tray. The usual amount of time it takes a print to reach its optimum development is somewhere between two and three minutes after the first appear-

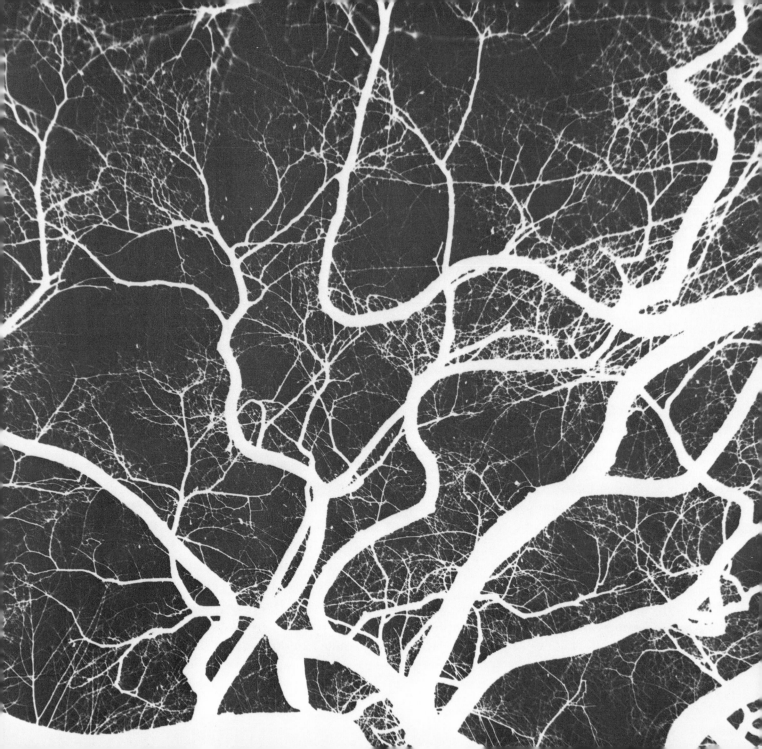

ance of the image, depending on what kind of developer you are using, as well as what kind of paper, and even what temperature the solution is. Pick up your fully developed photograph by one corner with your tongs and hold it over your developer tray until all the solution has dripped off it. Then drop it carefully into the tray containing the stop solution, being sure your tongs don't touch any of the solution.

5. Take hold of a corner again, this time with the second pair of tongs (it's good to have each set a different color to keep them in their own trays) and gently agitate the print under the stop solution. If you listen carefully you should hear a slight hissing sound which is the powerful hydrogen being released from the developing agents. When you hear the hissing stop, you know that your print has been neutralized and it is ready for the next tray. You need only keep your print in the stop solution about twenty seconds. Pick it up by the corner again, let it drip over the tray, and then drop it into the hypo or fixer. You can use the same tongs for both the stop bath and the hypo because they won't affect each other.

6. As we noted above, your print should soak for about five minutes in each of the two fix solutions, or ten minutes if you use only one fix solution, agitating it with the tongs every once in a while to make sure that the fluid moves into and out of the emulsion on your paper. Then on to the fresh-water wash and you are done. Once you take your print out of the last fix solution, you can turn the white light on again and see more clearly what you have accomplished. If all went well you should have a negative image of the scene you captured with your camera in the world of light a while ago.

7. Once your negative is thoroughly washed, you need only dry it between blotting paper, and then you are ready to *contact-print* it into a positive image just as you did with your shadow-graphs. This time, however, since you have a developing darkroom, you need only expose your positive paper to bright bulb light for two minutes instead of two hours, and then bring out your photograph by pushing *it* through the trays just as you did its negative brother.

So that's that. If you were successful in making your first photograph, I know that time did not even exist for you, and you now have a record of your seeing that you will cherish always.

Let's rest on that for a while. In the next chapter we will take up the four major improvements that have been accomplished in modern cameras, and how we can use them to become better photographers. We will be getting back into the darkroom again before long, not only to refine the skills we learned this time, but learn a few new ones as well.

5. Managing Light

Improving a Good Thing

Whenever light happens, it happens in every direction. If you look carefully, you will find each source of light sending out its energy rays in a total outpouring. The earth turns us to our morning and we are in a flood of light until evening. Turn on your desk lamp at night and the whole room is touched with brightness.

If only you could see the light rays themselves as they criss-cross back and forth, bouncing every which way. Hold up a piece of light-sensitive paper in this chaos of energy and the whole thing turns black.

Using a similar phenomenon as another example, imagine how it would sound if you could hear all radio waves at once, right now as they pass through your room: simply a chaos of noise! It is only because your radio receiver is made so that it can select one station's beam at a time that you are able to distinguish what it broadcasts.

Likewise, the tiny opening of your pin-hole camera takes in only one beam of light from the thousands that bounce from each point of your subject. And so

you can "receive" or photograph it. It is simply because the hole is so small that your camera works. The bigger the opening becomes, the more beams of light from each point can enter so that eventually they overlap and confuse each other, creating a chaos rather than an image.

The pinhole in your ball-camera "manages" the light for you. Think of the simplicity of that fact! People never believe that my little rubber ball-camera, with only a pin-hole aperture, can make a photograph. And yet we know that it does work. It does take hold of the light beams reflecting from the world before us, and it does manage to see in the way that we ourselves do.

You could go on making photographs with your pin-hole camera all year long, and go on getting better and better at it, too. There is a great deal of satisfaction in doing things well with simple tools. If you care to, stay with your first camera and make a collection of pin-hole photographs which you can be proud of and would want to share. Working with your pin-hole camera is not just a beginning in photography: it is also a complete experience in itself.

If and when you are ready to put aside your own self-made camera, it will be because you choose to manage light a little bit more. Usually the first thing you want to improve is the time it takes you to make an exposure. There is that problem of the smallness of your aperture necessary to make a sharp image: since it is so small it only lets in light a little at a time. If only you could let in the light in bigger doses and have a sharp image, too. It's something like sipping a drink through a straw or guzzling it down straight from a glass. Well, we have another discovery to help us: *the lens.* Found all around us even in nature, a lens is simply anything that can bend light rays. Water is the most natural lens we have, and probably the first one man ever noticed. Look at your feet while standing in a pool or a lake, and they will seem to have shrunk. Better yet, look closely through a dew drop on a leaf some summer morning. There you will see your whole field of vision brought together into a topsy-turvy, miniature world.

Whenever light rays pass at an angle through something denser than air, they are slowed down and bent. You can see this happening if you look through a drinking glass with rounded sides straight-up at arm's length. Use an empty glass first. How does it affect the image you normally see? Now fill the glass with water and view again. The image is upside down and reversed!

Take a look through the empty glass again. This time move the glass back and forth slowly. What do you notice? Parts of the image change in size, and its edges become slightly stretched or distorted because the light rays are being bent toward each other after hitting the curvature of the glass. When you fill the glass with water you make it so "thick" that the light rays bend even more. In fact, they bend so much that they actually criss-cross at a point between the glass and your eyes. When you see them, they have gone from top to bottom, from right to left and vice versa. If you slowly bring the filled glass toward your eye, you can see the crossing happen about three inches in front of your nose. All the rays converge at this point and then change sides.

After experimenting with a rounded glass, you might like to see what would happen if you used a straight-sided glass for your viewing. Try as many filled glass shapes as you can find as lenses. What happens in the glass when you walk toward something?

The most common solid glass lenses are found in eyeglasses or in hand-held magnifying glasses. I can remember that, as a boy, I used a small magnifying glass to burn my name into wood by "focusing" the sun's rays into a white-hot, blinding point of light. That was really writing with light! The lens gathered together an inch of sunbeams and sharpened them down to a fiery point no pen or pencil could ever match. I did not know it then, but that searing spot was the "criss-crossing" point where the sun was turned upside down.

30

31

32

Unlike the simple pin-hole which manages the light beams by limiting their entry into your camera, the simple lens embraces an armful of light rays and brings them to a sharper and brighter image by far. This gathering ability of a lens not only allows you to have a bigger opening in your camera to let more light energy in, but also focuses the rays, pulling them together and then letting them reform into a sharp image somewhere in mid-air just beyond the criss-crossing point. This place where the perfect image is reformed is called the *focal plane*. The spot in mid-air where the rays criss-cross is called the *focal point*. If you place a sheet of light-sensitive paper at the focal point, you will record a spot of light, but if you place it at the focal plane, you will record a sharp, upside-down and reversed image of what is before the lens.

If you want to have a faster camera than your pin-hole model, you will have to make use of a lens. I know some clever people who put together their own *simple lens* box-camera. They just took the pin-hole camera one giant step forward in efficiency. One end of a short cardboard tube was fitted with a magnifying glass. When the tube was inserted through the front of a light-tight box, it became a movable lens. They had also fixed a hinged back panel at the rear of the box which could be lifted up. By carefully taping a thin sheet of tissue paper across the open back, they made a simple focusing screen. When under a large black cloth draped over all but the lens, they could move the lens tube forward and back until the focal plane hit the tissue and the image became sharp. Next

44

they sealed the lens tube in the "focused" position to keep out the light and taped some light-sensitive paper to the inside of the back door before shutting the box up tight again. By uncovering the lens, they could permit light from their subject to be reflected into the box and onto the paper. It worked well. The trickiest part, of course, was timing by trial and error to get the best exposure.

Both this homemade, simple lens camera and its little brother, the pin-hole, have still another management problem: they can only make one photograph at a time. After each exposure you must unwrap the whole camera in the darkroom, take out the exposed paper and reload it again. To overcome this inconvenience, roll film was invented. Film has the same kind of light-sensitive, silver-salt coating on it as the paper we have been using, but because it is made of pliable cellulose, it can be rolled tightly around a spool. In this way enough light-sensitive material can fit in a camera to take one, two or even three dozen photographs before reloading.

Moreover, since film is a clear substance, it works as a far better *negative* from which to print. The paper negatives we have been using affect the light as it passes through their fibers, causing our positive prints to have a somewhat softened image. There is no reason not to be pleased with that particular effect. In fact, some photographers prefer to use paper negatives for that very reason. But often, if not most of the time, you will want to have as crisp an image as possible and to achieve that, film is essential.

You could certainly rig up a homemade camera to handle roll film instead of paper sheets, but it would take some ingenuity. I must admit that I never even made a try at it. Instead, I happily bought myself a manufactured camera years ago. If you share my feelings about constructing one's own roll-film camera, then I advise you at this point to do just what I did and buy yourself the best camera your budget will allow.

As you may imagine, manufactured cameras come in all sizes, shapes and prices. The simplest and least expensive camera you will find will not only have a lens of some sort and be able to take roll film, but will also have a built-in *shutter* to manage the letting-in of light and a *view finder* to help you aim at your subject. It is only after you have used a rubber pin-hole camera that you really appreciate these "luxuries" built into that basic tool we use when we want to write with light.

6. Exposure

33

The Simple Camera

One of the basic facts I have learned about myself is that I have a fixed capacity for food. If for some reason I leave the table without taking my fill, there is a feeling of a little roominess left over inside of me. And when I overdo by eating too much, I walk away with a sense of discomfort. But when I discipline myself and eat just enough, both my stomach and I are happy.

There is a very similar basic fact in photography: every silver-salted paper or film has its own fixed capacity for light. If you don't let enough light into your camera, your exposure goes hungry and your negative will be thin and weak. Let in more light than you need and your film will be overwhelmed, making your negative fat with silver. But take in just the right amount of light energy, as it bounces from the objects in front of your camera, and you will come away with a well-balanced rendering of the lights and shadows you see before you.

If you want to be a good photographer, you are not going to be satisfied with underexposures or overexposures. What you have seen and valued is worth capturing as a "correct" exposure. But how do you do that, other than by the old trial-and-error method we have been using with our pin-hole cameras? The answer is that you simply discover the *fixed capacity of light* of your film and then measure out just that amount of light for each exposure.

The first part is easy enough to accomplish. Every piece of manufactured silver-salted paper or film is given a rating number which tells you how fast it reacts to light. Some emulsions are made with billions of very fine crystals of silver salt so that they can catch every subtle degree of reflected light. Film with this kind of a coating responds more slowly to light and is therefore given a lower number. At the other extreme are emulsions which contain far fewer but much bigger and coarser crystals for use when not much light is present. Film coated in this way

reacts much quicker because of the size of each crystal, and so is given a higher "speed" number. There are, of course, emulsions that react to light at a variety of moderate speeds in between the very slow and the very fast.

As an example, let us go back to the light-sensitive papers we used in our pin-hole cameras. The American National Standards Institute (ANSI) rates a very slow contact paper such as we used earlier with a speed number of 6, and gives a fast enlarging paper the number 250. Using the slow paper outside on a good bright day requires about a one-minute exposure, while with the fast paper it would take only one second of light coming through the pin hole to create

a good image. Right now, light-sensitive films are available with ratings from ANSI no. 5 all the way up to ANSI no. 3000. You may notice that the ratings on some films are still shown as an ASA number instead of ANSI. Both, however, mean the same thing.

If you are wondering why light-sensitive emulsions are made in such varying speeds, just keep in mind all the varying kinds of light situations there are, as well as the many different subjects one might want to photograph — from mountains that stand still forever to splash-happenings which last only for the blink of an eye.

As we mentioned above, the slow, fine-grained emulsions have an advantage in their ability to capture every subtle tone of reflected light, while the faster, coarse-crystal emulsions tend to give you photographs that are "grainy" or speckled when they are enlarged. So if you want lots of fine detail, your best bet is to use a slower film with its thin coating of billions of tiny silver crystals. However, if you know you are going to be in a situation where there is limited light and some motion, a faster film would work better. Modern chemistry has enabled film manufacturers to produce moderately fast films from ANSI 100 to 500 which can also hold detail and so give you the best of both worlds.

The rating number that tells you just what kind of sensitivity a particular film possesses can easily be found on the description sheet that comes with every roll of film. The manufacturer gives you a lot more interesting facts on the sheet than just its "speed," and it is a good idea to read the whole thing. The more you read about the various tools of photography, the more you will know about what to do when the moment comes for doing it.

To find out the details about a particular light-sensitive paper, you will have to ask at your camera store to see the manual that describes what is available. The book will not only give you the speed ratings of each paper but also examples to show texture and tone. While you are in the store, I suggest that you browse around and ask every question that comes into your head. Most people who own or work in a camera store are photographers themselves and are very willing to share their knowledge. Try to get to them when they are not very busy so they will have time to show you all the wares, even if you are not buying at the moment. I was lucky enough to be given a leisurely tour of the complete darkroom operation in one establishment.

Once you have begun to understand the various fixed capacities for light in each type of film and paper, you are ready to go back to the world of cameras.

Basically there are two great families in the camera world: the *simple* cameras and the *adjustable* cameras. Any camera that has only one aperture size and only one shutter speed is considered a simple camera. A camera that has a number of lens openings and a variety of shutter speeds for your choosing is an adjustable one.

SIMPLE CAMERAS

Simple cameras have a number of advantages, not the least of which is their cost. Not only are they inexpensive, but because they are simple, there is less that can go wrong with them. In fact if something breaks inside, it's often cheaper to buy a new one than to fix it. Usually such a simple piece of equipment just wears out from use. But if you gave your pin-hole camera a lot of use and were making good photographs with it, you are certainly going to make good photographs with a simple camera no matter how little it costs. Besides, you should know by now that the main ingredient in the making of a good photograph is not the camera but you yourself.

The main disadvantage to simple cameras is that each has only one setting for aperture size and shutter speed, and are programmed for general picture taking. The manufacturers have set them to be used only with an average speed film on a subject an average distance from the lens in average lighting conditions. If you get slightly away from the average, you will begin having trouble making correct exposures. Your images will turn out a little too dark, a little too light, or just a little blurry.

One reason these cameras are kept simple is to keep them especially well-suited for rapid use — for ease in taking quick snapshots. The basic trouble here is that very little real "seeing" takes place when you are simply taking quick snapshots. You can use up a lot of film, but you don't usually accomplish much "writing with light." So, resist the temptation to use these simple hand cameras carelessly. Take the time to "see," and then make a photograph rather than take a snapshot.

Even though the recommended film, the aperture size and shutter speed are packaged to give you the correct exposures only of stationary subjects in bright light, there are ways to get around these limitations. So that you will be able to use a simple camera even more broadly than the manufacturer intended, here are a few examples of how you can deal with subjects and situations that are apart from the average.

At this point you ought simply to take the film you expose to your camera shop to be developed and

printed. As we go along, I will give you tips on how to get the most from this process and even how to do it yourself.

CAPTURING MOTION WITH
A SIMPLE CAMERA'S SLOW SHUTTER

Find a road where there is only moderate traffic. It's best to begin with fairly quiet local streets, rather than with super-highways where everything is apt to whizz by dangerously.

1. Standing on the sidewalk near the edge of the road, aim the camera at some interesting structure or tree on the other side. Hold your camera perfectly still and while sighting through the viewfinder (perceptor), try to "catch" a moving car or bicycle by pressing the shutter just as it comes into view. Since the shutter of a simple camera is too slow to "freeze" the motion of such a happening, the resulting photograph will show the shape of the car blurred right across the distinct and sharp shapes of the background. The contrast of this blurred image with the steadfastness of buildings or trees can make a very satisfying photograph.

2. This time, instead of standing close to the road, get far away from it. You might make an exposure shooting down from the highest window of a building overlooking it. While holding your camera still, look through your viewfinder at the broad view of the street below, and press the shutter when an interesting car or truck gets right into the middle of the scene. Because of the distance between your camera

36

51

37

and the moving subject, the image will not tend to blur on your film this time.

3. For the next experiment, go back down to the edge of the road again, but this time look up the road through your viewfinder at the traffic as it is coming toward you. When an interesting vehicle reaches the point where it dominates the scene, capture it by pressing the shutter. Because the light reflecting from all points of the oncoming car doesn't really move from side to side or up and down but just keeps coming straight into your camera, the image formed on your film is well defined. There usually is a slight enlarging aspect to the image in your photograph which will give a subtle feeling of motion toward you. It certainly shouldn't appear as if the car were standing still when you photographed it because, of course, it wasn't.

4. Still at the edge of the road, try one last experiment in capturing a moving subject. Instead of holding your camera still, try this time to click the shutter while moving your camera at the same speed as the passing car or bike. To do this you will first have to sight your subject through the viewfinder as it is approaching in the distance. Follow it with your camera in a smooth swinging motion, and release your shutter just as the subject sweeps by directly in front of you. This is called *panning a moving subject,* and to be successful you must start your camera swing early and be moving at the same speed as your subject when you fire your shutter. Practice on a number of cars and trucks before actually expos-

ing your film. Keep in mind that you want to start your swing, shoot your shutter and follow through all in one smooth, single motion. Once you get the hang of it, you will end up with photographs showing a relatively stationary image of your subject against a very blurred background. This blurring behind the car or bike will give an interesting sensation of motion to your image. Compare this last photograph with that of the first experiment in which the foreground was blurred and the background sharp. Even though your simple camera wasn't built to take pictures of moving things, with a little know-how and practice you can make its slow shutter manage light well enough to get some quite out-of-the-ordinary photographs. After all, there are many, many interesting subjects that go rolling, running or flying by on any given sunny day.

What about capturing things on not-so-sunny days, when clouds cover the sky or when the earth begins to turn away from the sun and light begins to fade? There still are photographs to be made even with a simple camera.

MAKING SATISFACTORY EXPOSURES
IN LOW LIGHT WITH SLOW FILM

As we mentioned, the film recommended for a simple camera is rated as fairly slow and intended for use on bright sunny days. Even though there is a lot to see and capture on a day filled with sun, we often have just as many interesting opportunities in moments of lesser light. Here are some projects which will give you experience in making the very best use of the light that's available.

1. Go out on a dark, overcast day with your simple camera and find a tree standing alone somewhere. Circle it from different distances until you find, through your viewfinder, an aspect that satisfies you. Then get down low enough so that you are looking up at the tree against a background of the overcast sky. Capture it there as a silhouette with the light pouring into your camera from behind the subject. Remember that the strongest light is always that ocean of energy streaking down from our sun, even through dark clouds in the late afternoon. There may not be enough reflected light bouncing off of things to make a good exposure, but there is enough *incident* light falling from the sky against which to make a sharp etching of shapes onto your film. Shoot up against an eastern sky in the low light of early morning and against the last gift of the sun in the west as we turn away from it for the night.

2. The manufacturers of simple cameras usually recommend the use of flash bulbs or cubes when taking pictures indoors during the day since roofs and walls prevent a good deal of sunlight from coming into our rooms. The problem with flash-bulb light is that it hits our subject straight on and eliminates the natural shadows that are seen when light comes from above or one side. Flash-bulb shots always seem "flat" and uncomplimentary because of this lack of subtle daylight shadowing that we are accustomed to seeing. So instead of using a bulb, place

38

your subject up close to a sunny window. On a good day there will be more than enough light reflected from most of your subject to make a good exposure, if you shoot from the side. I have found that window-light photographs have great impact when I have caught my subject half in and half out of the light. The trick is to find an aspect where the available light touches, reveals or outlines what you want to see, while the dark shadow hides the unnecessary.

3. Load your simple camera with a fresh roll of film and make photographs of subjects as they stand in low-light situations. Even though your camera's set aperture and shutter speed will not be letting in enough light to make a correct exposure on your film, the light energy that does enter causes a weak but real latent image within the molecules of the sil-ver-salts. When you are finished shooting the roll, take your exposed film to a camera store and ask to have it *pushed* in its development. This means it will be left in the developing solution longer than usual so that the chemical agents can free up an extra amount of silver grains. This "over-development" of your film should make up somewhat for your underexposure of it. If your negatives still come out a little thin, you will then have to request that a *high contrast* photographic paper be used to make your final positive prints. We'll get more into the subject of prints and developing in Chapter 8.

Using your simple camera in the lighting situations recommended by the manufacturer will give you consistently good exposures. Striving to make your simple camera produce satisfactory photographs beyond its limitations will give you the extra satisfaction of knowing a little bit more about how to master light. If and when you want to go even further and begin to gain almost complete control of light, then you must consider a better camera — an adjustable one.

Because the difference between a simple camera and an adjustable ·one is much like the difference between a two-wheeled bike and a sports car, there are some new tricks to be learned if you are going to use the more complicated one successfully. And they are worthwhile enough to merit a chapter for themselves.

7. The Adjustable Camera

There is an ancient saying which states that you cannot step into the same river twice. Our world is constantly turning, and all things are becoming forever different, forever new. This particular moment will never come again to this mountain, nor will this flock of wild ducks fly to meet such a morning tomorrow.

If you are going to try, photographically, to take hold of the variety of moments you see in the world, you have to respect this primary fact: the world is always changing. And because life is never constant, to be able to capture all you see of it requires a camera that can adapt and change as the day itself changes. That is exactly what a well-made adjustable camera has been designed to do — to be useful in all seasons, for all times, for all happenings. With the right film inside and with a knowing photographer outside, a modern camera can photograph anything the human eye can see. In fact, in some cases, it can even photograph images beyond human vision, such as the heat shapes made by in-fra-red energy waves, or the circling paths of starlight made as we spin through a winter's night.

Freedom to adapt your light-writing to the world's variety comes from the number of options provided by your camera. Instead of one lens opening, there is an *iris diaphragm* made of thin metal plates which can be adjusted to form a countless number of different-sized openings. And instead of only one shutter speed, you can choose to leave your lens open for days, or for an hour, or a minute, or a fraction of a second. There are shutters today which will remain open for only one two-thousandth of a second.

When you realize that you can set such a camera to any combination of lens openings and shutter speeds, you begin to see what a great variety of exposures is available for your choice. Such freedom comes at a premium, of course. A great deal of craftsmanship and costly material goes into a good adjustable camera, which its price tag inevitably reflects. For a photographer who is truly excited by

his seeing, such a camera is a worthwhile investment. My first camera was a borrowed one and my next one, which I still use, I bought as a great second-hand bargain from a reputable camera store. Today, this old camera is my most valuable possession, not because of its worth in money, but because of the incalculable satisfaction it has brought me.

When I was a small boy, I was sent by my grandmother to buy a pound of bologna and a pound of cheese from the grocery store. The butcher asked me if I wanted the meat cut in thick slices or thin, and I quickly said "thick," thinking that I'd get more that way. When I got home, however, my grandmother told me that "a pound is a pound no matter how they slice it." I then insisted that the butcher had made a mistake in weighing for he clearly had wrapped up twice as many slices of cheese as he had of meat. But again my grandmother pointed out that it was simply because the meat was *denser* than the cheese that a smaller package of it equalled the cheese in weight.

In just such a way, an adjustable camera slices up and delivers light to your film. On an average bright day, for example, your adjustable camera can slice the needed energy thick through a wide-open lens, or thin through a lens stopped down to its smallest aperture. If you choose the thick slice of light, you will of course have to shoot at a very fast shutter speed. The smaller lens opening will, accordingly, require that the shutter remain open longer. The main point to realize is that both combinations deliver the same quantity of light. A pound is a pound.

You will notice a series of numbers around the aperture dial of your lens. These are called *f-stop numbers,* and they indicate the light-passing capacity of various lens openings. The f-stop number stands for a scientific ratio between that particular lens' focal length (the distance from the lens to the film) and the effective aperture size; 1/2 of the focal length = f/2, and 1/4 of the focal length = f/4. In other words the smaller the number the larger the opening.

It takes a little while to get used to, but working with your camera will soon make its particular settings familiar to you. For example, the largest opening on my camera is marked f/2 and the smallest is f/16. Starting from the wide open stop of f/2, each f-stop number that follows progressively decreases the illumination. So my lens settings are: f/2, f/2.8, f/4, f/5.6, f/8, f/11, and finally f/16.

Since closing down the lens to each smaller aperture keeps decreasing the image brightness falling onto your film, you have to adjust your shutter speed so that your lens stays open longer for each decrease in order to keep the exposure power of the light always the same. If you look closely at the shutter dial on your camera, you will see speed numbers indicating this gradual increase in time. My camera's shutter speeds proceed from 1/1000 of a second to 1/500, 1/200, 1/100, 1/50, 1/25, 1/10, 1/5, 1/2, to finally staying open one whole second.

As we mentioned above, on an average sunny day with a fine-grained film (ANSI 32) in your camera, you can set your adjustable lens and shutter to slice the light energy a number of different ways while always maintaining the exact same quantity of light in each combination. Thus on my camera, a setting of f/2 at 1/1000 of a second approximately equals f/2.8 at 1/500, which equals f/4 at 1/200, which equals f-5.6 at 1/100, which equals f/8 at 1/50, which equals f/11 at 1/25, which equals f/16 at 1/10 of a second. A pound is a pound no matter how you slice it.

The next thing to realize is that we don't always have average sunny days providing us with light, rather it comes to us in all kinds of intensities. To say it most simply, just as bologna is inch-for-inch denser than cheese, so too is daylight much more powerful than bulb light. For example, using the same fine-grained film again, my own wide-open lens at f/2 need let in only 1/1000 of a second of daylight to give me a satisfactory exposure. Whereas, in my room at night with only a desk lamp burning, the same wide-open lens at f/2 would have to stay open for a full second to gather enough light energy to make a correct exposure. Moreover, if I should choose to close my lens down to its smallest opening of f/16, it would then take a whole minute to gather in enough lamplight to do the job. During the day even with my lens closed down all the way, I still would need only a small fraction of a second of sunlight.

This full minute of lamplight might seem at first

to be more than that 1/10 of a second of daylight, but comparing the exposures proves that they are both equal. Because sunlight is so dense with energy, it just doesn't take very much of it to equal that of the soft lamplight. One slice of bologna for every two of cheese.

EXPERIMENT 1.

Load your adjustable camera with a film that suits your particular day. If it is a bright sunny day, select a film whose speed is below ANSI 100; if an overcast day, choose one with a little bit higher speed; and if you are planning to shoot in deep shade or perhaps indoors, then get one with a speed of ANSI 400 or more. The fact sheet in the box of film will give you basic recommendations on where to set your lens opening and shutter speed for the particular light situation in which you find yourself. Instead of simply staying with that recommendation, try photographing your subject also at the f-stops just above and below it. Remember that as you open up your lens one f-stop, you must compensate by increasing your shutter speed one step too, and likewise when you go the other way. As you close down your lens from the recommended opening, you must slow down your shutter notch-for-notch to leave it open longer. The resulting prints should all have the same exposure, but if you compare them closely you should notice a subtle and surprising difference in what they show you.

EXPERIMENT 2.

The project above will bring you a beginning awareness of how your adjustable camera can become a very personal instrument in recording the subjects you see. By varying the lens opening you not only have a way of managing light but also a means of portraying just what is most significant to you in your seeing. Try this out: find a subject that satisfies you all by itself. Come in fairly close to it, but keep the background in your viewfinder, too. Focus carefully, following the instructions which come with your particular camera, and photograph it first through the smallest aperture possible. Use the method in Experiment 1 to work your lens opening and shutter speed down from the recommended "middle setting."

Next, without changing your view, photograph your subject again, this time with your lens as wide open as your shutter speed will allow, notch-for-notch. Your results will show your subject within two vastly different *depths of field*. With the small lens opening, almost everything in front of and especially behind your subject is recorded in acceptably sharp images. However, when you photographed through a wide-open lens, the subject alone is in sharp focus and everything else blurs out of distinction. In the first case your subject stands in the company of many other things; in the second, your subject expresses itself alone.

From now on *you* can decide just what part of your seeing you will write down with light. If you want to stress the singular value of your subject, and take it "out of the crowd," you can do so simply by photographing it through a wide aperture and capturing it within a very narrow depth of field. By using smaller and smaller lens openings, you can bring more and more of the background and foreground into sharper detail. Knowing this enables you to use your lens as a writer's tool. You can "put in" as much of the environment as you want. You are free to merely suggest what surrounds your subject, or include it all if you find it meaningful. You are the photographer: take control of your camera.

EXPERIMENT 3.

Sometimes, if not often, you will want to photograph something that is in a light situation not covered by the recommendations on your film's data sheet. In that case use your best judgment and *estimate* an exposure setting that you think might be accurate. Make that your middle setting and after you have made an exposure with that combination, make additional exposures on either side of it, keeping your shutter speed constant but adjusting your lens one f-stop greater and then one f-stop less.

This is called *bracketing*, and if you are more than a little doubtful of your first guess, you can shoot an even larger span by making a total of five exposures in all: your middle set with two f-stops above and two below. Conversely, if you are interested in maintaining the same depth of field, then keep the f-stop constant and bracket your shutter speeds instead. Re-

42

member to support your camera firmly if you are shooting slower than 1/25 of a second. Whenever you are photographing something that is special to you, it is a good idea to bracket your exposures. If what you see excites you, then you want to be doubly sure you capture a satisfactory image of it. You may not have the chance to go back and do it again if your first effort does not work out as you'd like. Both the subject matter itself and your own experiencing of it certainly make the few extra seconds and the few extra inches of film worthwhile.

What we have been doing all this time could be called "guess-timating" exposures, working them out through trial and error; building on the broad recommendations of the manufacturer, taking chances and sometimes almost "betting on all the numbers." I feel that doing this is all to the good. I especially want you to wrestle with light hand-to-hand each time you want to use it. This dealing with light on your own will help you become super-conscious of it in any given situation. And for someone who wants to become a writer-with-light, this keen awareness of light's presence is very necessary.

Just as I suggested in the use of the simple camera, continue "coming to grips with light" for as long as you like. Working with only the bare necessities will never hurt you. As long as you keep on working, it will only make you a better photographer in the long run.

EXPERIMENT 4.

When you are ready to take one more step toward

the mastery of light, and you have ten or twenty dollars to spend, consider buying yourself a *light meter*. There is just no way to avoid the fact that the earth is turning or the fact that our light is ever-changing. It is hard to keep up with light. Moreover, every single thing that stands in this tide of energy reflects light in its own unique manner. There is not only moon-shine, but there is also sea-shine and sand-shine, snow-shine and grass-shine, stone-shine and wood-shine, mountain-shine and sky-shine, even you-and-me-shine. After years of squinting at the various levels of light reflections I still, at times, "guess-timate" more light coming from my subject than there actually is and underexpose my film.

First of all, my eyes themselves are automatically adjusting to the light level all the time and, secondly, my brain is "generalizing" too much, trying to make things easier for me. So I end up seeing a little bit better than my camera, even when I don't want to. I have to admit that the only way I really know just how much light is bouncing off some particular object toward my camera in a given moment is to measure it with my light meter.

A light meter does two important things: it can accurately measure the *luminance* of light coming from a specific area; and, when adjusted to this reading with its dials set to the ANSI speed rating of the film being used, it can then display the entire string of f-stop/shutter speed combinations that will produce the correct exposure in that light situation.

There are some cameras on the market today which

43

44

are described as "totally automatic." These have light meters built right into them which alter the shutter speed automatically as the subject brightness increases or decreases. I find this type of camera undesirable not only because it can make "automatic mistakes" when subjects are standing against bright backgrounds, but especially because such locked-in automation takes all *personal* control out of your camera. As convenient as they might seem, they are really "aim and shoot" cameras designed primarily for snap-snap shooting and not for those interested in making photographs.

Far superior to the "totally automatic" are those cameras with built-in meters that just give you a reading of what light is coming into your lens and leave it up to you to adjust your f-stop number and shutter speed to a combination that matches its findings. This is popularly called a "match-the-needle" system and it is frequently found in a single-lens reflex camera. The real advantage here is that the photographer is able to measure the light actually coming in through his lens at the very moment he is composing his photograph in the viewfinder. The danger remains, however, in the tendency to match needles carelessly, without really considering which combination of f-stop/shutter speed you are selecting. One of the primary values of having an adjustable camera is being able to create with your lens opening that depth of field which corresponds to your personal visualization of the subject matter. Moreover, there is the basic necessity of al-

ways being aware of your shutter speed in relation to your subject's movement or even that of your camera. Use your camera as your tool; don't ever let it dictate to you. You are the one who is doing the seeing; the camera is only a very helpful box.

My preference has always been to use a separate, hand-held light meter. First of all, when I am looking at something my eyes unconsciously see each relative brightness that is reflected toward me. I see separate details and not just an average total light coming from one direction. So when I want to record what I am seeing, I find that a hand-held meter lends itself much more readily to noting these subtle differences and thereby makes me much more aware of a brightness range before my camera. Then by using an average meter reading of the reflected light coming from only the details I am interested in, I can set my camera to catch them.

Secondly, just having the complete read-out there in the palm of my hand is very helpful to me. The whole string of possible exposure combinations is in plain sight and, much more so than a built-in meter, a hand-held one asks me what is *my* choice.

Whether you buy a meter which is built in to a camera or buy a separate, hand-held one, be sure to read the instructions that come with it. There are many different kinds of light meters, but they all are quite simple gadgets once you learn how to use them. And that only takes a few minutes of explanation and a little bit of practice.

8.
Processing

46

Life Answering Life

In the last few chapters we have been concentrating on capturing images safely within little black boxes. Now I want to take you back again to that "second act" of photography; the rebirth or *processing* of your film into a new life and form. Retrieving those experiences which you visualized out of the blackness of your camera is still your responsibility for they are completely the product of your seeing, the offspring of your perception.

Picture-takers rely on camera stores to process their exposed film. They hand in their roll of snapshots and wait a week. When they come back, they simply pay their money and pick up their "jumbo" prints. The negatives are returned also, tucked away somewhere in the envelope, but they seem unimportant and usually go unnoticed as well as uncared for. The jumbos are quickly looked over (and we hope enjoyed) and then relegated to a drawer, or at best labeled and put into an album which is then put into the drawer.

I want your photography to have a much richer life than this. Even if you don't now have the money or the time to equip your own darkroom, there is still much you can do that will honor your personal responsibility to your photographs.

First of all, when you bring your film into the camera store, request that your developed negatives be returned with a *contact proof sheet* instead of jumbos. The proof sheet is simply made by exposing your negative strips to light directly against a sheet of photographic paper for a brief time. The result is a page of tiny positive images, the exact size of your negatives. Since this procedure requires only one sheet of paper and very little time, the cost is about one quarter of the standard processing charge. More importantly, the making of a contact sheet is done by hand and not by a snip-snap-roll-'em-out machine. This means fewer scratches on your negatives and much more faithfully produced images. You will notice that with the proof sheet, you get your negatives back within a neat *glassine* envelope.

Although at first glance a page of tiny prints may not seem to be a very practical form for viewing what you have photographed, it actually will prove to have many advantages over the alternative machine-developed pack of enlargements. With a proof sheet you have the chance to examine each frame exactly as it was shot to see what happened to each negative you exposed. *You* can decide which of them you would like enlarged and not bother with those that do not satisfy you. If you have been experimenting or bracketing your shots, you already expect that some will not turn out perfectly. A magnifying glass will help in making the choices and clearly seeing the results of your experiments. The self-discipline involved in searching your contact sheet for the "best of the best" will teach you as much from your mistakes as from your successes. And the personal care involved in this hand-picking of the photographs worthy of being enlarged will bring you much satisfaction when they are finally shared with others.

Not only can you select which individual photographs you want to single out, but you can also indicate on your proof sheet just how much of each negative you want printed. Perhaps there is an unavoidable but unwanted telephone wire across the top of your frame or a clutter of litter at the base. By carefully drawing a box with a grease crayon around just the part in which you are interested, you can *crop* out whatever detracts from it. Then, when you bring your selected negatives back to the camera store, simply request that they "enlarge and crop as marked" only those frames indicated on the proof sheet. You will also have a choice of size for the enlargements which will depend on how you want to display your finished photographs. A well-exposed negative can be satisfactorily blown up to a poster size of sixteen by twenty inches.

Whatever your decision about size, be sure to share the finished product in a way that does justice both to your subject and to your own personal moment of seeing. *Drymounting* a print neatly onto a styrofoam board is one simple and inexpensive method. You can buy a pack of drymounting tissue at the camera store; it is quite inexpensive, comes with easy instructions and requires only a regular household iron to do the trick. The board can be trimmed flush with the edges of the print and is so light that back-rolled adhesive tape will secure it to a wall. All sorts of frames, with glass or lucite, at all sorts of prices are also available in many different kinds of stores, including camera stores.

Be sure to put your negatives and proof sheet aside carefully for future reference and use. I recommend that you number and date the pair, filing the negative envelope in a dry box and your proof sheet in a separate three-ring binder. Soon you will have a useful chronological record of your photographic work, in which you can easily find a photograph you wish to print up by just looking over the pages of your proof sheets. When you locate the one you want, it will be simple to find its mate in the negative box.

You can also keep a separate portfolio of your fin-

ished enlargements for safe keeping. Keep in mind, however, that the best thing of all for your photographs is to be on display in order to be seen again and again. Why else did you care enough to write it down with light?

After the invention of books, they became so popular that not only were private libraries built, but also public ones were provided for everyone's use. The same is happening with photography. Making photographs has become so much a part of modern culture that many towns have at least one darkroom completely outfitted for free public use. You just have to know where to find them. As I mentioned earlier, the places to look for darkroom facilities are public schools and colleges, community centers, and especially local photography clubs to which your camera store can probably direct you.

If you have the time and the budget for your own developing and printing setup, then by all means complete the process of photography on your own. If you continue making photographs, you will save a lot of money in the long run, and besides, your total involvement will bring you a great deal of personal satisfaction: the photographs will be yours from start to finish.

BACK TO THE DARKROOM

Because you will be handling light-sensitive film, the process must take place in a darkroom. What you will need in order to develop roll film is really not very expensive.

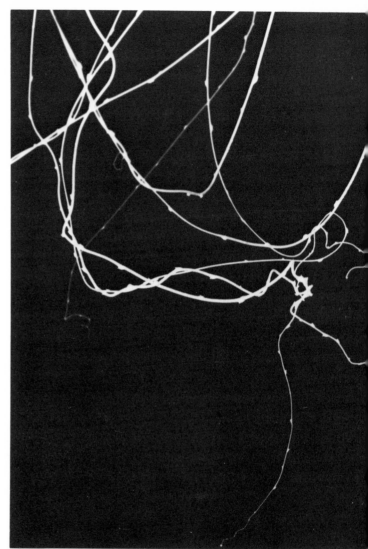

48

1. Most essential is a small *developing tank* designed for the size of your film. A developing tank is simply a light-tight container with either a reel or a long plastic apron for loading the film. The most ingenious feature of the tank is its light-tight cover. It has an opening that permits the pouring in and out of the various chemical solutions while the lights are on without exposing what is inside. For a beginning, you can buy an adequate plastic developing tank for just a couple of dollars.

2. Since the development of film has to be closely timed in relation to its speed rating and the temperature of the developing agents, you will need a *timer* that you can set manually to ring when the exact developing time is up. Camera stores sell them for under ten dollars, but a simple, less expensive kitchen timer will do the job for you, too.

3. Because the developing process is a chemical reaction you will have to control the temperatures of the solutions while they are working. This really is easy to do since the chemicals have been designed to work their best at room temperature. All you need is a simple *thermometer* and a two-inch-deep *tray*. By mixing warm and cool tap water you can easily get a tray-full that registers 68°F on your thermometer. Since standing water tends to maintain a constant heat level very well, all you need do is set your developing tank in the pan of water during the twenty-two minutes or so needed for the whole chemical process to take place.

4. As you recall, the whole developing process requires the three basic chemical solutions, *developer*, *stop* and *fixer,* and then a thorough washing with *water.* Film requires its own kind of developer which has a slightly different formula than what we used on our silver-salted paper. However, the stop and fixer solutions are the same, so there is no extra expense there. If you choose to mix your own chemical solutions, you will need three opaque bottles, but perhaps the best way in the beginning is to buy the agents already mixed in solution even though it will cost you a little more.

5. The only other items you need are scissors, a bottle opener and a cellulose sponge, each of which you may already have available.

DEVELOPING YOUR FILM

The whole procedure for developing film takes less than an hour to complete, and is just a four-step routine that you can perform on a table top by the sink in the darkroom.

1. Take the *dry reel* or apron out of the tank and place it aside while you fill your tank with the developing solution. It is almost impossible to load film onto a wet reel. Set your timer for the amount recommended on the data sheet that came with the film you are using. You will want to start it ticking away as soon as you place the loaded reel into the developing tank.

2. Since film is super-sensitive to light, this part of the procedure has to be done in *total* darkness without even a safe light. This means that you will have to place everything carefully within reach beforehand so

that you not only can find what you want in the dark, but also go through the necessary motions smoothly. I suggest that you simply arrange things from left to right in a line across your table: the sealed cassette or roll of exposed film, the bottle opener, scissors, empty reel, filled developing tank, the cover for the tank, tray of water and, finally, the timer ready to be started. When the lights are turned out, pry open your film cassette with the opener (if your film is in a plastic in-stamatic container, just break it open by twisting with your hands); take out the spool of film and cut off the short narrower leading edge with the scissors so that you have a squared-off end; then carefully thread the film onto the reel according to the directions given by the tank manufacturer; when fully loaded drop the reel slowly into the filled developer tank, cover it se-curely, start the timer and then put the lights back on. Rest the tank in the tray of room-temperature water.

3. Because little air bubbles sometimes cling to the film when it is being placed in the tank, the first thing to do once the timer is going is to tap the bottom of the tank against the table top three or four times to free them. Then gently agitate the solution within the tank by rocking it back and forth for about ten seconds. You want to have the developing solution actively working on every bit of your wound-up film through-out the entire recommended time span. For this reason you must repeat this gentle agitation every thirty sec-onds, continually bringing fresh developing agents into contact with each part of your film. When the timer rings, *do not open* the tank but just take off the pouring cap (if it has one) and empty the developer back into its bottle. Then pour the stop slowly in through the same opening, agitate it a little bit and empty it right back into its bottle. Finally, with the tank cover still on, pour in the fixer solution and let it fix your film for about ten minutes with some agitation every sixty seconds. Once you pour the fixer back into its bottle you can remove the tank cover completely since your negatives are now safe in the light.

4. To wash the negatives, simply place the open tank in the sink and let room-temperature tap water slowly run into the center of it for about twenty min-utes. After that you can unwind the long strip of nega-tives from the reel, being careful not to scratch the still soft emulsion or touch it with your fingers. The best way to dry them is to hang them on a line just like laundry. String a cord across your room and fasten the film strip to it with a clip of some sort at the top end. By attaching another clip to the bottom end you will help it hang straight and not dry curled. To make sure no water spots dry on the emulsion, wipe each side of your negative strip with a damp cellulose sponge.

That's it. All you need to do now is wait a couple of hours for your negatives to "harden" and then cut them to fit your glassine envelopes, which you can buy for a penny apiece at most camera stores.

FROM NEGATIVES TO PRINTS
What is the first thing you want to do with your nega-tives? Right. Turn them into positive prints as quickly as you can.

In the old days, photographers used large box-cameras that produced negatives which were as big as the cameras themselves. Contact printing positives from these large negatives was as simple a procedure as our making shadow-graphs at the beginning of our workshop. The large 8 x 10 contact prints they made in those days were very suitable for framing and viewing just as they were. But today's popular cameras all use rolls of miniature film. And that's why your negatives are the size of postage stamps and require another step called *enlarging*.

You have everything you need to perform this operation except one impressive piece of apparatus called the *enlarger*. Actually an enlarger is only a light bulb behind a lens. By slipping a negative between the light and the lens you can project an image onto paper to almost any size. It only depends on how far the lens is from the paper.

When you think of it, an enlarger works just the reverse of your camera. A camera uses light on the outside to carry the images of life through a lens into the dark chamber where the film waits. The enlarger puts the light in a box and throws the image from your negative back out into the world. Before, the mountain was out there and you used the magic of light and lens to get it into the box you held in your hands. Now in your darkroom, you can use light to project the mountain from its postage-stamp existence to a meaningful size which can once again bear all of its message to those who want to see.

Enlargers, like cameras, come in all shapes, sizes

and prices. If possible, purchase one that matches the quality of your camera. By that I mean, if you have a camera with a truly excellent lens, then the sharp negatives it produces deserve an enlarger with a lens equally as good. If, however, you are shooting with an average lens, you would then be wasting your money on an expensive enlarger, for no matter how excellent its lens is, it cannot create a sharpness that is not already present in the negative.

Since there is very little that can go wrong or wear out in an enlarger, buying a second-hand apparatus which should be cheaper makes a great deal of sense, not only for a beginner. Some of the old European models have very good lenses, and even though they may have a slightly antique appearance, they will delight you with their performance, In any case, make sure that the one you get is suited for the size of the film you are using.

1. Set your enlarger up on the dry table of your darkroom close to your safe light. You will also want some convenient place nearby to store your negatives and printing paper.

2. If you have not bought a *printing easel* to hold your paper flat under the enlarger's light, you can easily fashion one by cutting two 9 x 12-inch capital "L"'s out of heavy cardboard. By interlocking them head to toe like this — ⊡ — you can create any number of rectangular shapes as borders for your prints.

3. Before you place your negative into the enlarger's negative carrier, clean it carefully of all dust by brushing with a soft camel's hair brush. Each speck

74

of dust on your negative will also be enlarged and revealed as annoying white specks in your print. Be sure that you only touch negatives on their edges so that your fingers don't leave marks. The quality of your enlargements will clearly reflect the care you have taken with your negatives.

4. So that you can compose and focus your image before the actual printing, place a blank piece of white paper (not photographic paper) in your easel. Turn on your enlarger's light and turn off the darkroom light. Now open your enlarger's lens as far as it will go to provide as bright a projected image as possible. By adjusting your easel and by moving the enlarger head up and down, you can compose the photograph until you are completely satisfied. This is a very important moment in your work so don't rush through it. Take your time to re-create the image you visualized when you first experienced your subject. Consider whether you want to crop any areas out. Experiment with various formats, especially the most fundamental one: is the subject best expressed vertically or horizontally? When you have chosen the size and shape of your image, bring it to a fine focus by adjusting the small focusing knob that moves only the lens up and down. With this done, close down your lens to an opening of f/8 or f/11 so that your image's sharpness will be more increased.

5. When composition and focus are set, turn off the enlarger's light but leave the safe light on, and replace the plain white paper with a sheet of silver-salted enlarging paper, being careful not to move the easel from its determined place. Now you have to find out how many seconds of light passing through your negative it will take from that distance to expose a satisfactory image onto your paper. Find a piece of cardboard the size of your printing paper. After you have switched on your enlarger light, start counting out loud with an even beat, "One thousand, two thousand, three thousand, four thousand," etc. When you reach ten thousand, cover up one sixth of your paper but keep on counting. At twenty thousand, cover up another sixth of the paper. Continue covering another portion every ten beats. At the end of sixty beats when you turn off your enlarging light, you will have exposed your paper with six different quantities of light, varying by ten seconds each.

6. Still under the safe light, take your exposed paper over to the developing table and work it through the trays. You need not wash it for it is only a test sheet. Just give it a quick rinse with water once you have fixed it for a couple of minutes, and then turn on the room light for an examination. Looking at each test strip carefully, pick out the exposure time that satisfies you most. If you cannot make up your mind between twenty and thirty beats, for example, perhaps what you want will be found in a twenty-five-second exposure.

7. Once you have chosen the exposure time, all you need do is shut off the room light, re-load your easel with a sheet of fresh enlarging paper, and count off the exact amount of image light from your enlarger. Then put that sheet through the chemical trays, giv-

51

ing it a good fixing and washing this time. The end result should please you. If it is the first print you have ever made, you will remember it for years to come. Don't hesitate to dry it, mount it and display it somewhere quickly.

8. When looking at your finished print you may judge that it could be improved if only you could darken this particular area over here, or if you could make that shadow a little less dark. There is nothing wrong with trying to improve a good thing. The problem is, after all, a photographic one caused by the fact that film and paper are just not tolerant of the subtle tone contrasts that our eyes can distinguish. That area was not really that light when you saw it, nor was that shadow so dark.

Since it is a photographic problem, let's use photographic techniques to correct it and try a second print. First project your image onto plain paper once again but this time, with the enlarger lamp on, stick your hand or finger in between the lens and the easel so that it casts a shadow onto the image. By moving your hand or finger up and down you can regulate the size of the shadow you cast. Position your fingers so that they cast a shadow just on the area you want to lighten. If that area is located in the middle of your image and your hand casts too much of a shadow as it comes in from the side, you must then fashion a simple *dodging tool*. Cut out a circle of cardboard about the size of a quarter and attach it to a handle made of thin but stiff wire, about five inches long. Use this tool instead of your fingers to cast the shadow you want. If you keep the wire moving slightly while you are printing, it will not be seen in the final result.

Once you have practiced blocking light from areas you want to make less dark, do it with a fresh sheet of enlarging paper in the easel. Turn the enlarger light back on and start counting off the beats already used during the first exposure. After about five beats, begin dodging out the light from the specific area with either your hand or dodging tool for about five or six seconds. When you take your hand away, keep on counting until you finish your full exposure time.

If there was an area you wanted to make darker in the original print, then simply expose it alone for additional time. Do this by shielding the good area with the shadow of your hand and allow the light to burn in where you want a darker image. By using a little planning you can apply this trick of *burning in* to many separate areas of your image, building up lights and shadows as an artist does with his brush. Expose this area for fifteen seconds, this one for nineteen, and this background sky for fifty-five.

When you have completed your dodging and burning in, process the print through the chemicals and see if your improvements satisfy you. If not try again. On a sketch of your image, mark down the various exposure times you plan to use. In this way you will have an easier time keeping track of them when you are counting out the beats during the actual printing. An easy way to get your sketch is to trace over the projected image on a piece of plain paper, outlining the main areas you are interested in working on. You should keep this sketch as part of your record with your contact sheet. Someday you may want to make another print of this negative, and having the exposure times recorded will save making another test sheet.

As you work more and more on your prints you will slowly come to realize how much they are the creations of *your* seeing. Once, on a day now past, light revealed an interesting sight to you. You cared enough about that experience to take hold of it with your camera. Now you have brought it back into light to exist once more, this time as a photograph. Life is happening all around you on its own. Your photograph happened only because you chose to write it. It is certainly a part of life and it is certainly a part of you — of your seeing and of your photography.

9. Quiet Meetings

52

When I go out to photograph, I go alone. I take my camera, film and light meter, and for a few hours I give myself to walking and seeing. Though some of my friends have wondered whether this was a lonely hobby, it is really just the opposite. Although I seem to be by myself, what is happening between me and what I see is anything but loneliness. These quiet meetings are the beginning of my photography.

And now it is your turn.

Because our world is a genuine kaleidoscope of exciting images, I suggest that you set a definite course to discipline your search for visual values. For a start, try working your way through the following subjects: *the still, the free* and *the personal.*

THE STILL

The simplest and most persistent visual value you can find on earth is the rock. Geologists tell us that in the beginning our earth was all fire and movement, but when it quieted down enough for the evolution of life to start, hard rock began forming. From this process of cooling-down came the rains which eroded and shaped the rocks and made the seas salty. From these nourishing waters warmed by the sun came the first plants, the insects, fish, birds, animals and, man.

Seeing rocks standing resolute at the edge of the life-rich sea always speaks to me of this great odyssey of the earth. Such rocks are so clearly ancestral that when I meet them I feel an uncanny kinship with them, and I find it hard to break away from their spell.

Inland rocks have a power, too. Deep in the tall woods, a boulder may bear on its back a coat of green moss and purple lichen whose tiny almost invisible roots feed and take life from the rock's hard shell. The towering trees may have sheltered it from wearing rain, but someday one of them will drop a seed in that moist green bed and when it grows, its muscular roots will crack and crush the stone into humble earth. Such rocks are strong and sacred presences, and remind us that we are still at the beginnings of life.

A boulder, therefore, has real meaning as a place to start when seeking out still subjects to photograph. Find those which say something uncommon to you — something in that strange language uttered since the beginning of time.

To write down the very simplicity that is a rock, you will want to capture the finest details possible on your film. To do this, remember four things:

1. Slow films with ANSI numbers below 50 have billions of fine silver grains so that they can register a great many subtle tone differences. *If you look for detail, use the slowest-speed film possible.*

2. Remember that your camera's lens will transmit a much sharper image of your subject if it is closed down to a small opening. *For a photograph that is sharp and has fine resolution, use the smallest possible aperture setting.*

3. Since you will be shooting with a slow film through a narrow lens opening, your light reading will most likely demand that you use a slow shutter speed. Rocks by their very nature stand still, which eliminates part of the problem. But if you are shooting at a shutter speed slower than 1/30 of a second, you do have to worry about slight camera movements causing a blur in the image. *When photographing at slow shutter speeds, either use a tripod or brace your camera firmly on some stable object while releasing the shutter.*

4. Another hint: rocks tend to be quite reflective, so you must be careful of glare. It is usually best to photograph them on an overcast day, in shadow, or when the sun is low in the sky. Be sure to take a careful light reading and to bracket your exposures. The low angle of the sun's rays will reveal a great deal in shadow-relief across the rock's surface. *If a rock has an interesting texture you want to capture, try to photograph it with early morning or late afternoon light.*

Often a rock will say quite a lot all by itself, and you'll want to fill your whole camera with it: let it appear within your photograph all by itself. There are instances, however, when a rock stands *in relation to* its surroundings, and cannot be separated from the company it keeps. You will have to discover whether or not this is so by using your viewfinder as a perceptor. Keep an open mind so that you will be free to respond to the true perspective when you see it. *Keep whatever is important to your sight dominant in the photograph.*

Here again, early morning angled sunlight can be a great help in your light-writing. Photograph your boulder at different times of the day, in different kinds of weather and in the different moods of the four seasons. What stories your rock will tell you if you give it time. Part of the virtue of rocks is their patience. They are always available for your visits no matter what, and are always open to your study and touch.

They also seem to have interesting companions. If you look around them you will likely find other "still realities" to discover with your camera. Some fine day try to get in touch with the quiet presence found in delicate wild ferns or tiny mushroom families.

When you are photographing small subjects, you not

54 55

82

only want to get up close enough so that they can be felt in your composition, but also since they may be standing in a crowd of other subjects, you should consider photographing them within a shallow depth of field. Remember that to do this you should choose an exposure setting with the widest aperture possible. A photograph of a fern or a mushroom breaking up through winter's dead leaves makes a good spring gift. I do not think there was ever a photographer who was not moved at one time or another by the gentle call of this new life springing from a secret corner of the forest floor.

After a while, find an old tree standing in the middle of a field or at the very edge of the sea. There are trees which possess such strong qualities that it is easy to imagine people in the past worshiping them. These woody creatures are so much of the earth, and yet when their feathery branches are caught by the wind they seem almost ready to fly away. And when they are still and barren in the winter, trees are a naked geometry of life reaching out for life. Spend a lot of time with trees. They are very special.

THE FREE

When you have truly experienced the stationary world around your life, turn your attention to the world of movement and flight. Here is the song of freedom that Nature sings throughout the day. Once there were only still rocks and now there are birds flying overhead. Miracle happening!

Spend a day or two following the flight of birds only with your eyes and without your camera. Use your curled hand as a perceptor and try to distinguish the various moments in the rhythm of flying. It is a whole new experience, and if you are going to capture a brief second of flight, you will want to have the habit of seeing it happen. Tell yourself as you watch, "Now I would shoot, and now, and now." Look for these *decisive moments,* no matter how brief they are, when your visual instinct says to you, "now."

You could concentrate instead on the animal movements of cats, dogs or horses, for they too have a beauty all their own. But there is something exquisite in the flying of birds, and I would like you sometime to come to know it.

Sea gulls, or pigeons if you live inland, offer a good beginning point. Not only are their flight patterns particularly beautiful, but gulls and pigeons seem fond of soaring, with wings outstretched, through extended spans of time. They are also fairly tame and so will be apt to fly nearer to you than other wild birds.

Go to the shore at low tide when the gulls are feeding. They will often fly just a few yards over your head and if they are dining on clams, you can catch them dropping the shells to break open on the rocks below. At the moment they release the shells, they stand up on their tails in mid-air, giving you a fine display. They are forever chasing each other, too, swooping every which way in tandem.

Gulls like to face their beaks directly into a strong onshore breeze and hang on it almost motionless over the edge of the surf. When they spot a little tidbit on

the crest of a breaking wave, they simply fall straight down and grab it.

In your attempts to photograph these flight-happenings, you should try all the techniques of catching motion which I described in Chapter VI. You may prefer a little blur in the wings to carry the message of movement. If so, use an exposure combination that has a moderate shutter speed of 1/100 of a second. Another time, however, you may find the poetry in shape and feathers of a wing display worthy of being frozen in time. Here you will have to shoot at the fastest shutter speed that the light condition permits. And to catch a gull in full flight over the line between wave and sky, try some panning shots.

Much of the above also applies when photographing city pigeons, but because the background is usually composed of buildings rather than an open sea-sky, you will have a little trouble isolating the birds. Here again panning works best, for it will blur the buildings away. You could also position yourself to shoot up between the "canyon" walls.

As you probably know, hungry pigeons will gather right at your feet if you have some bread or nuts. Their movements on the ground are also very interesting to capture, particularly when many are gathered in one place. Try to catch a flock as they are all landing or, better yet, when they suddenly explode in flight. Perhaps the pigeon's most beautiful moment of flying is when he locks his wings and goes for a long, free glide down into the wind. See if you can capture some such moments.

THE PERSONAL

That which sets the *personal* above and beyond all else in our world is the power of language. Usually when we think of people and language we think of spoken or written words. These words, however, give only a very narrow view of what is going on in another person. I think you will find that it is often in *non-verbal* gestures and facial expressions that people communicate what is *personally* within them at that moment.

We are not used to "listening" to people with our eyes, which is probably why we seldom hear what they are really trying to say. To seek the personal in the life around you, look at people in the same way that you looked at rocks and trees. Use your camera as a perceptor and try to catch the unspoken language that is written in a person's face and posture. Something important is there, and you will be surprised at how clearly you will see or "hear" it once you begin trying.

You will probably be a little shy when you first point your camera at people, and that is understandable. You may sense that people are not as trusting as trees, and that they can object to your writing them down with light. I felt the same way when I began seeking personal images with my camera. To get used to the encounter I began by shooting statues in museums and parks. They were rich in human expression and gesture, yet were made of stone or metal so that I could have my way with them without fear. These photographs gave me a great deal of satisfaction and were

a good preparation for my later experience with real people.

Actually my transition from cold stone statues to warm human life took place in a museum. I began to notice people sitting and standing quietly concentrating on the art around them. Their own involvement in seeing left them unaware of my camera. It was an easy matter to slowly sweep my camera around until I saw a personal expression that said something to me. My shutter is very quiet and by simply continuing my sweep around in pretense of seeking something else, very few people ever knew I had been photographing them.

This made it not only less embarrassing for both them and me, but it also allowed me to capture them in a moment when they were simply being themselves. I could catch them thinking, talking, laughing, wondering — doing all kinds of things that rocks, trees and birds can never do. And yet, I could see such a naturalness about these human acts and expressions that they reminded me of the still reality I had been photographing all along. Visions of reality are all of the same family, only this time it was special.

Photographing people in this unobtrusive way in the midst of life is called *candid* photography. There is a rich personal honesty communicated in successful candid shots that just cannot be equalled with words. So when you feel you are ready for real excitement with your camera, take the step up to this higher plateau of expression and begin seeking the living human moments around you.

Working inside museums presents the challenge of low-light photography and usually requires a fast, wide-open lens, as well as careful use of a light meter. If you have a simple camera, try to catch people when they are in direct sunlight by a window or at least with a bright window behind them as a backlight.

When working outdoors in a park you have, of course, the great advantage of "light supreme" — that ever-present torrent of sun-energy. You will be able to shoot its powerful reflections at faster shutter speeds and more easily catch those fleeting expressions that happen once and never again.

When you begin looking for people in the park, start with the very young and the very old. The little ones are so occupied with their playing that they may hardly ever notice you. So uninhibited and so total is their involvement that they can portray the whole drama of humanity right before your eyes. They crawl about like snakes and go flying off like eagles; they sit still for long serious minutes and then march like an army only to play leap-frog among the trees; they scheme secretly and then shout out loud, laugh and cry like no other of God's creatures; they make very bitter war and then a very loving peace. And all in an hour's time!

Near the children, you can often find those who are retired from active life and who watch and remember. The gentle wisdom of the elderly will almost always accept you and your camera. They are well aware of what you see in their tired shapes and old faces. Some, in answer to the permission I sought with

58

59

my eyes, would hold up their heads as if to offer me a good book to read; others would turn aside to show me their faces in profile as if they were battle wounds. At those moments, they seem as tireless as old oaks, and yet tomorrow they can suddenly be gone from our seeing — but not entirely so if we gather the expressive light reflecting from their faces into our cameras.

When you have worked at capturing visions of the young and old themselves, turn your camera toward what happens *between* people caught up in the business of each other. They are in the act of communicating and sharing, and that is what being a person is all about. When you see it happening through the lens of your camera, you will know that you are witnessing life in its richest form.

Just as light is nothing for us until it touches something else, so a person becomes truly real for us only when we see him in contact with others. Sometimes the communication is so powerful an event that it becomes a third part of the scene in itself. This third part is the joy, anger, impatience or sympathy which you can almost see between two people in touch with each other. For the moment the third part lives its own life. Capturing this "in-between" with your camera is as thrilling as catching sun beams bursting out of a leaden sky.

These flashing moments demand not only our immediate reaction if we are to catch them, but also a camera that is ready to do the job. So get things set up ahead of time. Take a general light meter reading in the area where you plan to shoot. Choose a setting with a fast enough shutter speed to stop human motion and a small enough lens opening to provide you with a fairly extensive depth of field. By prefocusing at an average distance you will not have to fidget with dials when a special moment occurs. Just shoot, wind and be ready to shoot again.

After these photographic experiences with the personal life around you, try moving on to what is considered the most challenging photography of all — making a *portrait* of someone. In portraiture the personal contact is no longer between two people you see, but between one person and *you*. As a portrait photographer you are not simply a spectator; you must actually join in. If you are to be at all successful in making a portrait, your subject has to communicate himself or herself to you. That takes trust. From your side, you must be able to receive that personal message if it is given. That takes open-mindedness and caring.

There is a certain intimacy here which is much more direct than when you were photographing trees. You are as personally responsible for it as is your subject. Perhaps you are even more responsible than your subject for you are behind the camera, and you are not revealing much of yourself.

I began portraits by practicing on my best and most trusting friend — *me.* I hung a large mirror on a tree in a field when the light was right, and began trying to really see myself honestly. There was no question of what the truth of me was; I knew that, but it was not so easy to reveal it, even to myself. This technique

60

certainly made me sensitive to the personal generosity of a subject in a portrait. I have been grateful ever since when I have either received this gift or have been given the privilege of making it.

Here are some hints which you may find helpful

88

when you begin portrait photography. Even though most professional portrait photographers prefer to have their subject sit in a studio in which the lighting and background can be controlled, I have a consuming fondness for the truth that natural lighting gives. Moreover, I have found that most people are more relaxed and giving of themselves when they are in familiar surroundings. I try to get them in their own rooms either near a sunny window or with a tripod and ordinary room lighting. If they are agreeable and the day is good, I will also try to photograph them outdoors in some natural setting that seems suitable. We are so much a part of nature that the earth, trees and sky often help us forget our distractions and be ourselves.

Since light-colored clothing can sometimes compete with the quiet voices of faces and hands, I usually suggest that the person I am photographing wear something dark. The same goes for the background. If possible, keep it in contrast to the flesh tones. Decide how much of the background you want to keep and adjust your f-stop accordingly.

There is nothing more subtle than the human personality, so do not hesitate to study every aspect. If a mushroom deserved your close attention, how much more do you owe to a person?

Bring lots of film. As the encounter between photographer and subject develops, you will discover more and more. Many times I have felt that I was getting close to catching the real person only to run out of film.

If ever you find yourself in a portrait session where it becomes obvious to both of you that nothing true is being revealed, take a break and switch roles. Let your subject photograph you for a while! Give of yourself, and perhaps when you get the camera back you will finally receive.

61

Conclusion

62

There are times out-of-doors when I unexpectedly come upon what seems to me at that moment to be a unique wide vista. All at once everything is united there before me, from the most distant horizon right up to the ground at my feet. Sky, clouds, hills, rocks, grass and me. Big and small, high and wide, far and near, all becomes one when seen from this spot at this time. I see it as a super-abundance, and feel it as overwhelming in its goodness, in its promise.

Trying to express with words what is experienced in such moments somehow never makes it. Music at times comes close but it, too, is a little inadequate. We have really needed a new kind of language to help us share what we see when we truly do see: that new human language is photography.

All of us are just learning our ABCs in photography: all of us are still beginners. Some of the first photographers on earth are still alive. And yet, so powerful has been the work from their cameras that already our generation prefers to see than to read.

The fundamentals I have learned in photography, I have passed on to you. Go see things for yourself now. Go seeking alone early in the day when sunlight gives its greatest revelations. Walk in places that are open and give yourself completely to your eyes. There is nothing on earth that can see as personally as you can. Find the simple and the super-abundant. Celebrate it: write it down with the light that is given to you. Share it with your friends. And teach them, too, how to see and how to write with light.

NOTES ON THE PHOTOGRAPHS
(Unless otherwise noted, all photographs were made by the author.)

Jacket. A simple shadow-graph made by two students placing their right hands on fast enlarging paper: ten-second exposure with an overhead incandescent light bulb in a darkroom: developed and fixed chemically.

1. A portrait made with the indirect sunlight reflected within a room on a December morning: Leica camera: Tri X film: 5 mm lens: f/2.8 for one-second exposure.

2. A candid shot at close range in November midday sunlight: Leica: Plus X film: 50 mm lens: f/8 for 1/500-second exposure.

3. Photographed at midevening by Conn O'Neil: Canon Reflex camera: Tri X film: 50 mm lens: f/5.6 for 4 seconds with a tripod.

4. Very early morning sunlight captured by Conn O'Neil: Rolleiflex camera: Tri X film: 75 mm lens: f/16 for one-second exposure with a tripod.

5. Another aspect by Conn O'Neil: same place, same time, same data.

6. A late afternoon western sky in early December: Leica: Plus X film: 50 mm lens: f/11 for 1/25-second exposure.

7. Overexposed by Conn O'Neil in late afternoon summer sunlight, then printed on a fast paper: Canon Reflex: 50 mm lens.

8. Candid shot by David Carvin on a summer afternoon: exposure forgotten but we remember burning in the shadows while printing on polycontrast paper.

9. Shadow-graph made the same way as the jacket print.

10. Simple shadow-graph made by placing an old typewriter ribbon on top of fast enlarging paper: same exposure as jacket print.

11. Same idea, but this time the portable typewriter was placed on the paper and exposed to light.

12. A shadow-graph by Conn O'Neil, made by filtering the light of an enlarger through a green stained-glass wine jug onto a fast enlarging paper: f/8 for ten seconds.

13. Double-exposure shadow-graph by Conn O'Neil, made first by exposing his hands through a piece of textured glass pressed on the paper, then by holding the glass five inches away from the paper and exposing it alone.

14. A shadow-graph of gull feathers placed right on slow contact paper at the beach: dipped in salty seawater to temporarily fix the print.

15. Subject pressed under glass and exposed for ten minutes in my back yard: processed the same as above, but fixed in a hot salt bath in the kitchen.

16. Another photograph by Conn O'Neil of sunlight coming in from outside: Rolleiflex: Tri X film: 75 mm lens: f/16 for one-second exposure with tripod.

17. Diagram of a ball camera by Chris Harris.

18. A photograph made with a pin-hole camera by Conn O'Neil on a spring morning: Tri X sheet film: pin hole made with no. 25 sewing needle: two-minute exposure: developed chemically.

19. A different aspect of the same tree: same pin-hole camera, same film, same exposure.

20. Another pin-hole photograph made with the same camera, this one with a one-second exposure: again developed chemically.

21. A negative print made from a positive slide transparency: exposed with an enlarger onto high contrast paper.

22. An egret in flight captured in the late afternoon spring sun: Leica: Tri X film: f/8 for 1/500 of a second: greatly enlarged grainy effect.

23. Paper negative of my father with early morning summer light coming from behind him.

24. Positive of the above.

25. Shadow-graph by Conn O'Neil as in no. 12, above, this time with a paper negative alongside.

26. Shadow-graph of my Capricorn glass paperweight on poly-contrast paper using the light of an enlarger: exposed for 45 seconds.

27. An overcast winter sky with no shadows captured by Conn O'Neil: Canon Reflex: Tri X film: f/16 for 1/25-second exposure.

28. Paper negative of elm-tree branches against a winter sky.

29. Photograph by John Rathe with summer midday light: Kodak Signet: Plus X film: f/11.

30. Reeds against the snow on an overcast winter morning: Leica: Tri X film: f/5.6 for 1/50 of a second.

31. Late morning light: Leica: Plus X film: 50 mm lens: f/11 for 1/250 of a second.

32. A candid taken by Conn O'Neil: Rolleiflex: Tri X film: 75 mm lens: f/4 for 1/30-second exposure: the resultant thin negative was then printed on high contrast paper.

33. A close-up shot by Conn O'Neil using mid-morning sun coming indoors through broken glass: Rolleiflex: Tri X film: f/8 for 1/30 of a second.

34. A summer seascape through a hazy, early afternoon sky: Leica: Plus X film: 50 mm lens: f/11 for 1/500-second exposure.

35. A tree against a late afternoon sky: printed on high contrast paper.

36. Falling water caught by Conn O'Neil: f/22 for 1/60 of a second: resultant thick negative required much burning in for shadows.

37. A panning shot of my son David made with a simple Insta-matic camera.

38. Silhouette against an early morning overcast sky, by Dennis Weller.

39. Natural light coming through an eastern window on a winter morning: Leica: Tri X film: 50 mm lens: f/4 for 1/25 of a second.

40. Patience rewarded. Wild ducks caught in early morning flight: Leica: 50 mm lens: f/11 for 1/500 of a second.

41. Candid of children on a summer morning: exposure forgotten.

42. Mushroom family close-up in the early morning woods: Leica: Plus X film: 50 mm lens: f/2.8 for 1/250 of a second.

43. Redwing blackbird swooping into a willow: Leica: f/8 for 1/500-second exposure.

44. Close-up of Queen Anne's lace back-lit with afternoon summer light: lens wide open.

45. Candid of children under overhead incandescent bulb light: Leica: Tri X film: 50 mm lens: f/2.8 for 1/25 of a second.

46. Shore birds flying into a sea breeze on a very bright day (thick negative), caught by Conn O'Neil: Canon Reflex: Tri X film: f/16 for 1/500 of a second.

47. Contact proof sheet containing 36 frames, showing some bracketed exposures and cropping notations.

48. Negative print of a vine against the open sky, made from a positive slide transparency.

49. An Amish road photographed by my wife on a summer afternoon: exposure forgotten.

50. Close-up of a gull feather in a tidal pool, shot with slow film (ANSI 32) under a bright overhead sun: f/5.6 for 1/500-second exposure.

51. A sea gull frozen in flight in midday sunlight: Leica: 50 mm lens: f/8 for 1/500 of a second.

52. Rocks at the edge of the Pacific Ocean: Leica: Plus X film: f/8 for 1/1000 of a second.

53. Detail of a rock, wood and flowers on the California coast under an overcast noon sky.

54. A gull in flight: Leica: Plus X film: 1/250 of a second exposure.

55. Same as above but exposed at f/8 for 1/1000 of a second and greatly enlarged.

56. An egret turning in flight against a late afternoon western sky: Leica: Plus X film: 50 mm lens: f/11 for 1/250 of a second.

57. Candid on the Brooklyn Bridge shooting up against a noon sky: Leica: 50 mm lens: f/8 for 1/250 of a second.

58 Whispering caught in the park in the late afternoon sun: f/5.6 for 1/500 of a second.

59. Noon napping on a park bench, photographed by John Rathe: 35 mm camera.

60. Afternoon break for summer workers on a bright day, by Conn O'Neil: Tri X film: 50 mm lens.

61. Close-up by Conn O'Neil on a dull, overcast day: Tri X film: 135 mm lens: f/16 for 1/125 of a second.

62. Late afternoon clouds filtering the last of the sun's rays: Leica: Plus X film: 50 mm lens: f/11 for 1/50 of a second.

63. Vista of a California valley: Leica: Plus X film: 50 mm lens: f/16 for 1/250-second exposure.

Jacket back. Portrait of the author taken in the late afternoon by Jordi Viladas: 4 by 5 Crown Graphic View camera: Plus X Pan Professional sheet film: f/3.5 for 1/25 of a second.

ACKNOWLEDGMENTS:

No man is ever alone in his work, and I want here to thank those who have stood before, beside and behind me, helping in so many quiet ways to make this book be:

Everyone who shared their seeing with me during the past ten years of photography workshops . . . especially Dennis Weller, John Rathe, Jordi Viladas and Conn O'Neil, some of whose photographs appear upon these pages.

A fellow photographer, Charles Stephenson, who, knowing of my work, generously gave me much of his private collection of photographic books and journals. His gift has enriched and will continue to enrich many new photographers.

My kind and patient editor, Chris Harris of Chatham Press, who believed so much in seeing that he filled the pages of this book with photographs and not just printed words.

My parents whose gentle love brought me into the light of day.

Most of all my wife Anita and our four children who are the five most beautiful and precious persons my eyes have ever beheld.

8592

DATE DUE

Sauigner			